A History of Germany

PALGRAVE ESSENTIAL HISTORIES
General Editor: Jeremy Black

This series of compact, readable and informative national histories is
designed to appeal to anyone wishing to gain a broad understanding of
a country's history.

Published

A History of Spain *Simon Barton*
A History of the British Isles (2nd edn) *Jeremy Black*
A History of Israel *Ahron Bregman*
A History of Ireland *Mike Cronin*
A History of the Pacific Islands *Steven Roger Fischer*
A History of the United States (2nd edn) *Philip Jenkins*
A History of Denmark *Knud J. V. Jespersen*
A History of Poland *Anita J. Prażmowska*
A History of India *Peter Robb*
A History of China *J. A. G. Roberts*
A History of Germany *Peter Wende*

Further titles are in preparation

A History of Germany

Peter Wende

First published 2005 by
PALGRAVE MACMILLAN
Houndmills, Basingstoke, Hampshire RG21 6XS and
175 Fifth Avenue, New York, N.Y. 10010
Companies and representatives throughout the world

PALGRAVE MACMILLAN is the global academic imprint of the Palgrave Macmillan division of St. Martin's Press, LLC and of Palgrave Macmillan Ltd. Macmillan® is a registered trademark in the United States, United Kingdom and other countries. Palgrave is a registered trademark in the European Union and other countries.

ISBN 0–333–68764–7 hardback
ISBN 0–333–68765–5 paperback

This book is printed on paper suitable for recycling and made from fully managed and sustained forest sources.

A catalogue record for this book is available from the British Library.

Library of Congress Cataloging-in-Publication Data
Wende, Peter.
    A history of Germany/Peter Wende.
        p. cm.—(Palgrave essential histories)
    Includes bibliographical references and index.
    ISBN 0-333-68764-7 (cloth)
    1. Germany—History. I. Title. II. Series.
    DD89.W46 2005
    943—dc22   2004058395

10	9	8	7	6	5	4	3	2	1
14	13	12	11	10	09	08	07	06	05

Printed in China

Germany is a queer country: one can't regard it dispassionately
(D. H. Lawrence, 12 August 1914)

Contents

CONTENTS

List of Maps

Preface

When, a couple of years ago, Jeremy Black as editor of the Essential Histories Series asked me whether I would agree to write a concise history of Germany, my first thought was to decline the offer because of my poor English. But at the same time I was tempted by the challenge to present the history of my country to an Anglo-Saxon reader who might associate it mainly with the horrors of the Nazi period and the dissolution of the GDR, or with the names of Otto von Bismarck and Kaiser Wilhelm II. That is why I finally decided to accept – because the task was different from writing a history of Germany for a German public or even for my learned colleagues. And I can only ask my British and American readers to excuse my sometimes faulty and often clumsy English.

An even greater problem was how to squeeze a general history of Germany from the Romans up to the present day into a single 200-page volume. Concentrating on what I regard as the essence of German history has necessarily involved me in taking historical short-cuts, reducing complex developments to short summaries or cursory generalizations, and sometimes even skipping over whole periods.

I was prepared to take this risk because I did not want to try to give a strictly narrative account, but wanted instead to make it clear that it is impossible to give a straightforward history of Germany. To me, writing a history of Germany means searching for 'Germany'. The aim of this little book is to show that throughout the course of the last 2000 years German history has, in fact, been the history of many Germanies, and that it can be written neither as the history of a region nor as a political, ethnic or cultural formation.

Even a brief glance at the maps of what has or might have been called 'Germany' throughout the ages reveals the fluctuating patterns of kaleidoscopic alternations in shape and composition. Though there are elements and lines of continuity, the history of Germany has been the history of nearly constant change. This is why I have preferred a sequence of portraits of the different Germanies to a largely chronological narrative, and why I have concentrated on periods of crisis and turning points.

The main theme of the book is the development of Germany as a national and political entity, and this necessarily implies the discussion of general points of political, economic and social history at the expense of other aspects of current concern of some modern historians, such as gender or the family. As I have concentrated on the essentials and main characteristics of German history – a history which is in many aspects more complex than that of the other major European nation-states – I will only touch on social, cultural or gender history when it is linked to some characteristic aspect of German history (for example, the role of the Prussian nobility).

Naturally, this book is not based on primary research but relies throughout on the often stimulating work of earlier historians on various aspects of German history. And because the notes as well as the bibliography had to be kept to an absolute minimum, all I can do here is state that I am most grateful to those who by their research helped me form my own view of the history of Germany. My special thanks go to my colleague Andreas Fahrmeir who helped me with the difficult job of selecting and redrawing the maps.

Should the book claim any originality, then it lies in the selection, arrangement and presentation of the subject matter. As I could not possibly aspire to provide a complete account of the unattainable whole, I tried to map out a framework for what I consider the essential topics of German history since it is my aim to stimulate curiosity, to encourage further interest in the subject. Should anyone, after having read the book, say or think: 'Now I know all I need to know about the history of Germany' I would have failed. But as soon as he turns to the suggestions for further reading, eager to study German history more closely, I would be satisfied with my job.

Peter Wende

1

Origins and Beginnings

A ROMAN PROVINCE

On the hilltop of a wooded mountain ridge in eastern Westphalia, near the provincial town of Detmold, towers a huge monument: the statue of a warrior clad in a short tunic, brandishing a 23-foot-long sword and gazing sternly out from under his winged helmet towards the south-west. It was erected to commemorate Arminius, a noble member of the Germanic tribe of the Cherusci, who led his warriors to a decisive victory over three Roman legions in the year AD 9.

Today we know, thanks to recent excavations, that this battle took place in the swamps and forests of the region near Osnabrück and not near Detmold, and that it was more of a mutiny by Germanic auxiliaries than a fight for freedom against Roman oppression. Still, since the time when German humanists started to invent a German national identity, for many this battle has been the starting point of German history and Arminius became '*Hermann*', to some even the real person behind the Siegfried of the *Nibelungenlied*, that famous German epic poem of the thirteenth century. And thus when nineteenth-century German nationalism was at its height shortly after the victory over France and the formation of the German Empire in 1871, the erection of this monument was to symbolize the myth of the origins of the German nation-state.

However, that part of central Europe which was to become Germany was not restricted to those wild and desolate lands east of the Rhine and north of the Danube, which Tacitus labelled 'Germania'. And, accordingly, no ethnic or cultural unity can be established either. In the west and south there were the Roman provinces of Germania, Belgica and Raetia, bordered by the rivers Rhine and Danube, and in between the *agri decumates*, i.e. the region protected against raids by the Teutonic peoples from north of the border by the *limes,* a huge bulwark of palisades and fortifications running from the Rhine near Koblenz to the Danube near Regensburg.

Here, over two centuries of Roman settlements laid the foundations of a cultural heritage which was to become a formative factor in German history. Numerous towns, among them Augusta Treverorum (today's Trier), which for a period ranked among the leading cities of the empire, stone buildings, market places, a network of roads, luxurious *villae rusticae* (the country houses of the Romans) and extended vineyards demonstrated the prosperity of the region. And even when, from the middle of the third century onwards, the barbarian raids from the north became more frequent and more devastating, until the Roman defence broke down at the beginning of the fifth century and migrating Germanic peoples started not only to plunder and to conquer but to settle, the cultural divide remained. There was also a second borderline, the one in the east between the Germanic and the Slav peoples.

The region where the formation of Germany took place can thus be divided into three zones: Germania Romana, Germania Germanica and Germania Slavica. And these zones again encompassed not cultural uniformity but infinite regional variety. Patches of fertile soil, more numerous in the south and west, formed rather densely populated islands in huge seas of wooded or swampy wilderness. Among them the most important were in the Rhine valley round Cologne, near Frankfurt and Heidelberg and south of the Danube near Regensburg, and they remained economic centres on the economic map of future Germany.

In the beginning there was no Germany and there were no Germans. In the beginning there was Europe, that is, those parts of western, central and southern Europe which at the time of Charlemagne's death in 814 formed the Carolingian Empire.

THE CAROLINGIAN EMPIRE

After the decline and fall of Roman power in Western Europe the Germanic people of the Franks, who had repeatedly harassed the province of Gallia since the middle of the third century, finally crossed the Rhine in the year AD 406, in the wake of the great German migration. After their Merovingian King Chlodowech (466–511) had won

2

the last battle against Roman forces in 486, he and his successors started to expand their rule slowly but steadily. In the end, during the long reign of Charlemagne (768–814), it stretched from the North Sea to the Bay of Biscay and from the English Channel to the Adriatic. At the same time, the rule of King Charles signalled the emergence of a new empire, for, at Christmas 800, the Pope crowned him emperor: *imperator romanum gubernans imperium*. Three centuries after the last emperor in the west had been deposed, the Roman Empire had been resurrected with the aid of the Christian Church by transferring the title of emperor to the most powerful ruler in Western Europe. Henceforward the seal of the ruler bore the words *renovatio imperii romani*.

However, unlike its Roman model this new Carolingian Empire was not to last for centuries. Though Charlemagne tried hard to create a widespread administrative network for the peoples under his rule, making use whenever possible of the relics of Roman institutions and the spreading universal network of the Church, in the long run this huge domain was doomed to fall apart. One of the reasons was its sheer vastness, which made efficient communication impossible: sending a message from Aachen to Rome would take three months. Moreover, severe problems were caused by the customary rules of hereditary succession.

There was no rule of primogeniture by which the heritage would be passed to the eldest son. Instead, according to Salic Law all the legitimate sons were entitled to an equal share of their father's estate. And it was only due to chance – to the fact that two of his sons had died before him – that on his death in 814 Charlemagne could leave his realm undivided to his last son, Louis 'the Pious' (778–840).

But, in spite of all the emperor's efforts to preserve the unity of the realm, the empire was to break apart after his death. After the murderous battle of Fontenoy (841) Charles the Bald and Louis 'the German' forced their brother, the Emperor Lothar I, to grant them their share. The treaty of Verdun (843) sealed the division of Charlemagne's empire. Charles was to inherit the western part, Louis the domains in the east, and Lothar to keep the lands in between, from then on called 'Lotharingen', i.e. Lorraine, as well as the Italian kingdom. Finally, when his line died out, Lorraine, in a piecemeal process, fell to the eastern Frankish kingdom. The treaty of Ribémont defined the frontier between the two kingdoms and throughout the Middle Ages it remained more or less unchanged.

Although (as a result of the chances and accidents of lineage and succession) Charles the Fat was once again sole ruler of the empire for a short time between 884 and 887, the process of dissolution was irreversible. It demonstrated the failure of the attempt to preserve the unity of the empire by establishing a multiple kingdom – the division of power and the partition of the realm finally led to separation. Charlemagne's empire did not mark the beginning of a 'second Rome' but it was the cradle of future European nation-states. There was a kingdom in the west which was to become France and another in the eastern and southern parts of the former Carolingian realm from which the medieval German Empire evolved.

Here, with the death of Louis the Child (911) the Carolingian line became extinct because he was not succeeded by a blood relation. Instead, the powerful nobles in the east decided to establish a new dynasty by electing Conrad, Duke of Franconia and still of Frankish origin, as their king. When he was followed by Henry I, Duke of Saxony, the last links with the Carolingian dynasty were severed. This has usually been regarded as the beginning of German history. There was still no Germany and there were still no German people. There was, however, a new kingdom which was to be linked to an empire and which, in the long run, turned out to be a major factor in the long process of the ethnogenesis of the German people.

THE EMERGENCE OF A GERMAN PEOPLE

The new kingdom which emerged in the eastern half of the old Carolingian Empire was not the political organization of a specific ethnic group. And although a kind of language barrier between the west and the east was slowly evolving – in 842 the two kings Louis and Charles swore a solemn oath in front of their armies in different languages – there was as yet no German people to form a German state. It was rather the other way round: this kingdom in the east, which was often still called *regnum Francorum*, or sometimes *regnum orientalum Francorum* – the eastern Frankish kingdom – provided the political frame for the gradual formation of a German people. And it was a long time before this medieval kingdom became a German Empire (*regnum teutonicum)* whose inhabitants were Germans and lived in Germany. People rather regarded themselves as members of one of the five ancient Germanic tribal units – the Franks, Swabians,

Saxons, Bavarians or Thuringians – which were later organized in the so-called 'stem-duchies' and together provided the basis of the kingdom.

These tribes had their own laws and their own dialects which, though related since they all stemmed from a common Indo-European source, still stood in the way of a common German language. Communication, not only in a European but also in a wider German context, still depended on the knowledge and use of Latin. On the other hand, the term *thiutisk* (Latin *theodiscus*) existed, which later became *deutsch*, but this originally just meant any vernacular of the common people set against the Latin of the learned clergy. It was not until the late eleventh century that the usage of this word was narrowed down to signify the dialects of the common German people. And because of this original connotation, for a long time the term related the name of the Germans to images of uncouth barbarism.

This points to the fact that even before the Germans started to call themselves Germans, they were called Germans by their neighbours, rivals and enemies. The Italians in particular spoke of *i Tedeschi* when the emperors from north of the Alps led their motley armies towards Rome. And in the course of his struggle with Emperor Henry IV, Pope Gregory VII used the label *regnum teutonicum* in order to reduce the universal claims which up to then the German kings had associated with the imperial crown to which they aspired. In 1160 the English clerical scholar John of Salisbury asked the famous question: 'Who has made the Germans (*teutonici*) judges of the nations?' in response to Emperor Frederick I's policy of unseating and enthroning popes according to his political preferences. In contexts like this, the term *teutonici* pointed back to the *furor teutonicus*, the horrors of the first incursions by warlike Germanic tribes into Italy in 102 BC.

And, indeed, it was abroad, far away from home, as members of an army in a hostile country, that German warriors from different German regions first experienced a sense of solidarity and community. Here they were not only called 'Germans' but also called themselves 'Germans' when they took the oath to keep the peace among themselves or when they gathered in common prayer.

At the same time the consciousness of and efforts towards a common language gradually began to emerge in Germany. Within an empire which in the Middle Ages included parts of France such as Burgundy and Provence as well as northern Italy, this group of German-speaking people formed the nucleus for the evolution of a

5

German nation. And even when a learned cleric like the historian Otto, Bishop of Freising, pointed out in the middle of the twelfth century that a German empire had emerged with the reign of Otto I, he also stressed the importance of the Carolingian tradition and the fact that the Germans were German Franks (*Teutonici orientali Franci*) and their empire of Frankish origin (*Francorum regnum orientale, quod teutonicum dicitur*), even if their kings came from a different family and spoke a different language.

Thus Germans were late to develop a common identity because they lacked a common ethnic substance and – initially – a common language. They achieved this goal in the end by means of a common history, that is, by the common institution of a kingship, which constantly united the different tribes and peoples in common endeavours, and finally in the common goal of an empire which in itself extended far beyond the boundaries of Germany. The outlines of a difficult beginning and the history of a complicated ethnogenesis foreshadow future developments in the evolution of a nation which differed so much from its neighbours that it always had to struggle either to overcome or to justify those differences.

2

. . . .

Medieval Germany

KINGS AND EMPERORS

One of the major factors in the process of the formation of Germany was the office of kingship, which decisively contributed to the integration of Germany as a political entity. In Carolingian times, according to traditional custom and contemporary understanding, monarchy was the natural form in which human society should be organized. Only the rule of kings, based on the chain of command and obedience, could guarantee law and order, peace and protection. Where there was no king there was no constitution and not even a realm. The king did not represent the kingdom or empire: he, or rather the power he wielded, incorporated the realm. Where there is no king there is anarchy and chaos. The kingdom (*regnum*) is not a certain territory within clearly defined frontiers but the totality of kingly rights and the whole of the sphere where he wields his power.

The position of the kings was further strengthened by the Christian faith and the Church. And whereas in Carolingian times the king was still regarded as God's servant (*minister*), later, in the time of the Saxon emperors, he was thought to act as 'the deputy of the supreme judge' and as God's proxy even within the Church.

But such high ideals of kingship would, of necessity, often clash with the harsh realities of medieval society. For where there was no standing army and no central administration at the king's command, real power rested with those who controlled the regions: the local magnates and their masters, the nobility. In fact, medieval kings would not and could not rule as absolute monarchs, but only with the consent and aid of their peers, the great magnates of the realm. The secret and the essence of royal power rested with the king's capacity to harmonize, unify and concentrate the real forces of medieval society, that is, to ally himself with the nobility and the Church.

To achieve this, medieval rulers were constantly on the move. This was especially so in Germany, where, since no capital developed, there was no place like Paris or London which could grow into a political centre and which would eventually become the main seat of royal power. Therefore, German kings and emperors not only travelled repeatedly to Italy, but north of the Alps, too. They continually moved from place to place with a huge entourage of up to 2000 persons, either holding court at royal palaces on the scattered crownlands or staying at the seats of mighty nobles, usually bishops. This continuous royal progress served as the essential means of 'government', of communication between the king and the nobility of the realm.

This fundamental alliance between Crown and nobles found its expression in the election of the king, which became firmly established within the political structure of the eastern Frankish kingdom, i.e. of Germany.

In 987, in the western part of the former Carolingian Empire, Hugo Capet succeeded in founding a royal dynasty which was to reign on the basis of hereditary right (including the sidelines), well into the nineteenth century. But here, in the course of the first two centuries after Charlemagne's death, the influence of the Crown was more and more reduced by the growing power of a new aristocracy which, apart from the king's domain in the Isle of France, divided the rule of the realm among themselves. Thus they were no longer interested in controlling the Crown by exercising their right of election.

In the east, on the other hand, the election of the monarch became a fundamental principle of constitutional practice. Along with the fact that early on the rulers here succeeded in rejecting and cancelling the principle of dividing the realm among all the sons, this grew into a unifying factor in the new kingdom and a lasting constitutional feature of the German empire for the next 800 years.

In the beginning, election did not necessarily mean selection, for example, from a number of possible candidates. The term would usually imply mere confirmation or acknowledgement or elevation to the high office of king. Quite often, as in the case of Otto I, the ruler's eldest son, who was already designated as his successor by his father, was solemnly 'elected' by the nobles of the realm. As a rule, possible candidates had to be members of, or in some way linked to, the family of the ruling king. Even in case of rebellion against the king, the principle of election applied, and the rebel nobles usually elevated a rival king of their own choice.

Thus the election of the king operated as a social contract for the political nation, that is, for the great magnates whose interests constantly joined with the interests of the realm on the occasion of the ruler's death. And thus at first this served as an element of stability for the new kingdom in the east, though later this usage would play its part in the process of the general decline of royal power. As royal dynasties frequently became extinct in the direct line, more than a dozen noble families had at least one member elected to the kingly office in the course of only four centuries. And with the growing powers of the aristocracy, the principle of election first weakened and finally destroyed the framework of hereditary succession, which for so long had provided the guidelines for the electors.

In 1077 the opposition against Henry IV proclaimed for the first time their right to elect freely a king of their own choice. In 1125, after the death of Henry V, this right was exercised with the election of Lothar III and, finally, after the death of the last emperor of the Staufer Dynasty in 1250, succession by election became a governing principle and distinct mark of constitutional custom in the German Empire. And now the chances increased for the electors to elect either a weak king or to bind their vote to grants and concessions by the future ruler in order to secure or increase their own power and position.

At the same time, the right to elect the ruler had always been a privilege of the leading nobles of the German realm, until from 1257 onwards it started to become restricted to only seven princes who made up the Council of Electors (as it was finally put down by imperial law in 1356). Its original members were: the archbishops of Mainz, Trier and Cologne, the Duke of Saxony, the Counts of Brandenburg and the Rhineland Palatinate and the King of Bohemia and, apart from some minor changes, this electoral body was to stay until the dissolution of the German Empire in 1806.

A second feature of medieval kingship which was to act as a forceful factor in German history was the link between kingdom and empire. From 962 onwards, when Otto I was crowned Emperor by Pope John XII in Rome, German (East Frankish) kings claimed to be the true heirs of Charlemagne because they possessed the military strength to act as the true defenders of the Roman Church. Though this did not provide the king with additional resources to deal with the extra tasks now on the agenda, it nevertheless implied a distinct elevation in rank in comparison to the rest of the Christian rulers of Europe. This spectacular extension of prestige corresponded to the natural aspirations of medieval kingship, and henceforth the main object of the policy of German kings was to realize their claim to the imperial crown, which could only be achieved by coronation in Rome. To assert this claim, as soon as he was elected, the German king called himself *rex Romanorum*, king of the Romans.

In the tradition of Charlemagne, the Empire included the kingdoms of (Northern) Italy and Burgundy and stretched from the frontier with Denmark in the north to Sicily in the south, a distance of more than 1000 miles. And though the German kingdom remained the source of their power, the political interests and aspirations of the emperors were focused on the lands south of the Alps, on the wealth of the urban regions of Northern Italy and on Rome as the capital not only of the Roman Empire but of the Christian Church, still regarded in the Middle Ages as the *caput mundi*, the centre of the world.

Therefore German kings not only led their armies across the Alps but also spent more and more of their time in Italy, as did the emperors of the Hohenstaufen dynasty: Henry VI and Frederick II are buried in the cathedral of Palermo. In the nineteenth and early twentieth centuries German nationalist historians were furiously to condemn this kind of policy, which drained the resources of the German 'nation' and in the end contributed decisively to the decline and fall of 'the first German Empire'. But the medieval emperors could not, of course, be expected to act according to the interests of a non-existent future nation-state. Instead, the aims of their imperial policy complied with the expectations of their contemporaries: they tried to achieve the first goal of a medieval ruler – to amass glories and to augment their honour.

As a rule, huge armies, sometimes up to 15,000 men, invaded Italy whenever the emperor decided to march towards Rome. For the Italians this often meant a revival of the *furor teutonicus*, as there was pillage and plunder in the wake of many hostile encounters. But considerable costs and risks were also involved on the German side, especially for the nobles who under feudal law were obliged to render military service. Apart from the dangers of war, unknown diseases lurked in the swampy regions of Italy and in the heat of the Mediterranean sun; many an imperial army was suddenly decimated by the outbreak of an epidemic and forced to retreat. On the other hand, rich booty could be brought home and apart from direct gains a

Map 1 Medieval Germany (adapted from Diether Raff, *History of Germany: From Medieval Empire to the Present* (Oxford, 1988), p. xii).

general cultural transfer from the south to the north was one of the main results of the emperors' 'Italian policy'.

However, in spite of the fact that between 1000 and 1250 Italy increasingly became the focus of German emperors' policy, the

German and the Italian kingdom, as well as Burgundy, remained separate units within the empire, preserving their special identities. Now, for the first time, the outlines of national identities can be registered, marking the location of future fractures within the empire.

In spite of repeated endeavours to connect the rule of the medieval emperors to Roman traditions, Europe did not become a 'Second Rome', for the other kingdoms in Europe never acknowledged the German emperor's supremacy and always stressed their right to meet him on equal terms – another milestone on the long road towards a Europe of nation-states.

On the other hand, in the nineteenth and twentieth centuries the memory of the medieval empire would haunt the politics of the modern German nation-state, for then German nationalism often claimed to revive the goals and aspirations of medieval German emperors.

A distorted view of medieval Germany played a decisive role when later German politicians and historians set about inventing a German national tradition from which a claim to a leading role or even hegemony in central Europe could be derived.

KINGS AND BISHOPS – EMPIRE AND PAPACY

In the Middle Ages there was no genuine successor to the Roman Empire which had forged Europe into a political unit, but there was the Church. It spread and administered the Christian faith, which soon unified Western, Northern and Central Europe and Italy. It possessed its capital, Rome, its head, the Pope, its own organization (with the diocese as the administrative unit) and its army – the priests and monks. It cultivated Latin as the common lingua franca in the sphere of European religion, politics and culture and it preserved manifold links to the heritage of ancient Rome, its literature and its arts. And thus its monasteries and cathedrals became the centres for education, science and scholarship. After the decline and dissolution of the Carolingian Empire it was the Church which served as a communication network stretching across all political, ethnic and geographical frontiers.

The realm of religion could not be totally separated from the realm of worldly power. On the contrary, both spheres not only touched but were closely connected and even interwoven because of their mutual need: the Church needed the protection of kings and nobles, and emperors and kings the network of the Church. Since 799, when Charlemagne defended Pope Leo III against his enemies by force of arms for the first time, emperors had repeatedly secured the safety and independence of the head of the Christian Church against attempts by Roman noble families to encroach on or even usurp the papal office. On the other hand, Charlemagne was also the first not only to protect the Church but also to control it, making use of it as a most valuable instrument in the administration of his realm.

The Saxon and Salian kings and emperors followed this example. After failed attempts to govern with the aid of members of his family, whom he had appointed as dukes of the realm but who, nevertheless, soon endeavoured to establish and extend their own power, Otto I turned the bishoprics into the main pillars of his rule. Nobles in the role of lay administrators always tried to turn the powers of their office into the assets of a family heirloom. Bishops and abbots, however, did not gain their seats by inheritance but by election and appointment which, up to the reign of Henry III, were mostly controlled or even directly implemented by the king.

The German part of the empire comprised six archdioceses – Mainz, Cologne, Trier, Salzburg, Bremen and Magdeburg – and 34 bishoprics. Besides these, there were numerous monasteries, the most powerful among them being St Gallen, Reichenau, Fulda, Lorsch and Hersfeld. Many of them were founded by the king or at least endowed not only with lands and immunities but also with substantial royal privileges such as the right to collect tolls, mint coins and hold markets. Thus bishops and abbots wielded not only spiritual but also worldly power when they exercised the rights of the ruler over great parts of the realm.

This integration of the Church into the sphere of royal and imperial power was demonstrated by the fact that large sections of the Saxon and Salian emperors' armies consisted of the military contingents of bishops and monasteries. In the tenth century 3000 out of 10,000 knights were supplied by the clergy.

The obligations of military service – that of appearing at the king's court, the performance of various commissions required by the king – weighed more heavily upon the persons and lands of the Church than upon the lay nobility. To achieve this close co-operation between Crown and Church, the latter was integrated into the feudal system of rights and duties which formed the backbone of what might be called the medieval form of government. Here the lord granted his vassal protection in return for service and in order to enable the vassal to render military service, for example, he endowed him with property. On this principle a pyramid of personal relationships was erected, with the emperor as its supreme head and the great nobles of the realm as his chief vassals. Within this system the Church formed an essential part, if not the main pillar, of the medieval German Empire. Bishops were as much part of the feudal hierarchy as they were of the clergy. They were lords of territorial principalities which equalled the duchies in size and power. Emperors up to Frederick I used the high clergy as commanders of armies, as diplomats, as governors.

At the same time, the Empire came to be regarded as the mould for the unity of Western Christendom, especially after the definitive separation of the Latin Church from the Greek Church in 1054. And at the height of their power, at the beginning of the eleventh century, the emperors did not act only as protectors of the Holy See in particular and the Church in general, but also as God's lieutenants on earth. Henry III treated the papacy as he would a bishopric. When, in 1045, there were three rival popes in Rome, the Emperor called a synod at Sutri, where all three were deposed, and afterwards he appointed a German bishop as head of the Church three times – a blunt exhibition of imperial control of the Holy See.

But in the long run the dual character of the Roman-Christian Empire, as well as the close co-operation between Church and royal government within the German realm, became the source of future conflicts. Tension became obvious as soon as the question arose as to who was actually acting as God's representative on earth. Was it the emperor as successor to his Christian Roman forerunners whose realm since 1157 had been named 'sacrum imperium' (Holy Empire)? Or was it the Pope, the bishop of the Roman See and head of the Church of Christ, from whom the emperor received the honour and power of the imperial crown and thus, by the act of the coronation, became the vassal of the Pope, as Gregory VII, Alexander III, Innocent III and others would argue?

At the same time, the growing involvement of the Church in worldly affairs was criticized. Soon a concept of ecclesiastical reform spread from the monastery of Cluny in Burgundy throughout Europe, which stigmatized all forms of secular control of church offices as 'simony', that is, the corrupt and hence forbidden custom of buying and selling ecclesiastical offices and privileges. When this argument was turned against the German emperors' usage of appointing bishops and investing them with their worldly as well as their spiritual power, the axe was laid at the root of the power of the Crown. By questioning the king's right of control over the Church through the prohibition of lay investiture, the whole edifice of royal government was jeopardized.

Thus when the concept of moral reform of the Church was linked to the question of church independence, the supremacy of secular authority was challenged, especially when this claim was taken up by the papacy in its struggle to free itself from the control of the emperors. The whole of Europe was affected by this clash between the two main forces of medieval society: kings and priests. But the decisive battle took place within the Empire as here the two antagonists met face to face.

Here the conflict culminated in the so-called 'War of Investiture' during the reigns of Henry IV and Henry V and was then continued in the lasting struggle between the popes and the emperors in the period of the rulers of the Hohenstaufen dynasty. It was a long and bitter struggle with dramatic highlights, such as Henry IV kneeling in the snow in front of Canossa castle in 1077 in order to be absolved from excommunication by Pope Gregory VII, or the lonely death of that pope in Salerno in 1085, uttering his last words: 'I have always loved justice and hated injustice and that is why I die in exile', or the conquest and ruthless sacking of Milan in 1162 by Frederick I, or Frederick II imprisoning more than 100 prelates on their way to a council in Rome summoned by Pope Gregory IX in 1241.

During the first stage the Church gained partial victory. In 1059 Pope Nicholas II established the College of Cardinals as the instrument for future papal elections, a device by which the Papacy could be freed from legal control by the imperial authority. In 1122 at a council in Worms compromise was reached with regard to the appointment of bishops within the German church: from now on the Emperor, who could still exert some influence on the election of the new incumbent, would invest him with the signs of the secular authority of his office while the Pope did the same with regard to the spiritual side.

In 1268 the Pope had obviously won a complete victory when his ally, Charles of Anjou, had young Konradin (the last descendant of the Hohenstaufen dynasty) executed. The link between Italy and Germany, established by the vision and tasks of Empire, was severed. For the next decades the Empire sank into chaos while in 1302 Pope

Boniface VIII in his bull *Unam Sanctam*, claimed world dominion for the papal See, only to be imprisoned by the French king in the following year. The so-called Babylonian Captivity of the Papacy in Avignon until 1377 and the Great Schism (1378–1417) proved that it was not the popes but their allies who were the true victors in this momentous struggle: the French monarchy, the great municipalities of Northern Italy and the German nobility, especially the princely rulers of the nascent territorial states.

THE RISE OF THE PRINCES

Aristocratic rule formed the backbone of medieval European society. It was based on the power of a small minority whose members had considerable landed property as well as bands of military retainers at their disposal so that they were able to claim their share in ruling the kingdom. This was the heritage of the great migration of the Germanic peoples, which had offered successful warriors the chance to acquire power over land and men. And, therefore, in the beginning all European monarchies were aristocracies with a monarchic head, where the power of the nobles at least counterbalanced the power of the king. The history of medieval politics is largely the history of the changing fortunes in a continuous struggle between the centralizing forces of the Crown and the efforts of the nobles to retain or even extend their own independent precincts of power.

In the beginning of the history of Germany there was a Carolingian imperial aristocracy. Its members were nobles in the king's entourage and he tried to use them as instruments of royal administration. As commissioners of Charlemagne some had been sent to newly conquered territories in the east and here, in Bavaria, Saxony, Franconia, Alemannia and Thuringia, the region of ancient Germanic tribes, they established the king's power, which they later managed to turn into their own power. As dukes (*duces*) at the head of new tribal unions they stood for the establishment of regionalism instead of centralism. Within a few generations, the delegation of royal power led to the rise of regional noble dynasties which, as they were often related to the royal family, soon laid claims to the high offices of the realm, thereby reversing the original relationship between office and nobility. At the same time they tried to close their ranks against upstarts and newcomers, thus paving the way for the rise of a hereditary aristocracy. These were the princes and dukes who in the course of the next few centuries were often to influence the course of German history so decisively.

But there was still a long way to go until the German Empire became a patchwork of princely territorial states. The main basis of princely power was land, held either as freehold (*allod*), or commissarially or administratively, or granted in feudal tenure. Yet those lands – manors, fields and forests and meadows, church lands, and sometimes even counties – were far from being consolidated territories. And, moreover, princely dominion embraced a welter of claims and rights such as mining and minting prerogatives, stewardships of monastic foundations, grants of market franchise and various jurisdictional rights which could be exercised quite independently of any control over territory. And, finally, status and power could also spring from ancestral fame, the number of retainers, the rank of the vassals, the pomp and splendour displayed on various occasions, such as a visit of the royal household.

At the same time, the pattern of regional strongholds of princely power changed continuously. Not only were possessions, rights and properties widely scattered, never forming a single solid block, but because the princes still regarded their lands as patrimonies, partition again and again severely affected certain dynasties, because until the late sixteenth century primogeniture rarely prevailed.

An exception to this was Germany's ecclesiastical principalities. They had grown out of the German emperors' attempts to turn the members of the higher clergy into pillars of imperial policy and administration. Therefore they had been richly endowed with lands, rights and privileges, which over time formed the basis of that unique feature of German history: ecclesiastical territorial states. Here partition posed no threat, for they were unaffected by dynastic succession. But though the incumbents were either appointed or elected, they were usually also members of the nobility and in the course of time the ecclesiastical principalities were dominated by the special interests of dynasties of the high aristocracy.

Medieval Germany thus was a complicated, partly chaotic, and ever-changing web of regional and local forces and interests, marked by continuous strife. Every duke, count and even minor noble not only tried to assert and consolidate but also to strengthen his position. Among these the most powerful was the king, whose task it was to establish and enforce law and order and to this end he had to expand

and strengthen his own power. At the same time he had to try to commit the nobles to his policy, to bind their interests to those of the realm. This he did by offering them a share of power through delegation.

The feudal systems provided the means for integrating the nobility into the structure of the Empire – the princes were endowed with fiefs and offices by their king in return for paying homage to him as their lord. But soon the hereditary principle absorbed the essence of feudal relations, turning obligations and duties into rights and privileges when the king was no longer able to take back what he had once handed out as a fief to his vassal. Though the princes had a share in power and politics by participating in the election of the emperor and administering imperial rights, the main object of their interest remained the extension and consolidation of their lands and rights.

Important milestones on the path to this final goal, the formation of a territorial principality, were the castles erected by many nobles from the eleventh century onwards, often in blatant violation of the king's monopoly on military strongholds. As fortified seats of the noble families, who soon began to add the names of these locations to their own names, they signalled the nobility's intention to achieve political independence and dominance in certain regions by concentrating their own power there. Thus, on the other side, emperors, too, had to try to expand and consolidate the lands and rights of the Crown as well as their own family heirlooms. And, indeed, at the close of the Middle Ages, only dynasties such as the Habsburgs, who commanded extensive resources, could successfully aspire to the office of king and emperor. Continual conflict between the Crown and the great landed nobility thus became the hallmark of medieval German history.

An impressive example of this tendency took place in the summer of 1073, when a group of Saxon and Thuringian nobles conspired and rose against King Henry IV to press the demand that castles recently erected by the Crown should be razed and lands allegedly unjustly confiscated should be restored. The wars that followed lasted for 16 years and marked the beginning of many further outbursts of rebellion against imperial rule. These gained in momentum when they were linked to the great war between Empire and Papacy, for the rebellious princes soon became allies of Pope Gregory VII and his successors. Whenever the pope excommunicated the emperor the great vassals were released from their oath of allegiance and could feel free to elect and support a rival king, who would serve as the focus in their struggle against imperial supremacy. Finally, the Emperor lost his case, because he had to fight on two fronts. In Italy he lacked the full support of the German princes and at the same time his Italian policy drained his own German resources, so that, in the end, he could not but succumb to the demands of the nobility. In April 1231 Emperor Frederick II, in the famous *statutum in favorem principum* – the statute in favour of the territorial princes – transferred the exercise of regalian rights and privilege in their domains to the princes, who were now no longer supposed to wield power at the king's command but rather in their own right.

At the same time, however, those princes remained as *princes imperii* members of the Empire (*membra imperii*), and as such they represented the highest order under the king in medieval society. According to feudal law they occupied the first estates within the social pyramid because they had received their tenures directly from the king. They gradually closed their ranks against other members of the nobility and enjoyed a number of special privileges. At the close of the reign of the Staufer dynasty in the middle of the thirteenth century this estate of the imperial princes (*Reichsfürstenstand*) comprised 90 ecclesiastical princes and only 13 temporal magnates, but their number increased considerably during the late Middle Ages, as a result of elevations by the Crown, until it nearly equalled that of the spiritual lords.

One should not overlook the fact that at the beginning of the fourteenth century, apart from the territories of these imperial princes, at least a third of the land was ruled by lesser nobles, non-princely counts and margraves, barons and knights. Such noble families of the second rank actually dominated certain regions of Germany, especially the heartlands of the empire such as the Rhine–Main area, Franconia and parts of Swabia, as well as Thuringia or northern Hesse. And though they had failed to consolidate their estates into a royal fief whose integrity was legally sanctioned by imperial law, these dynastic territories in administrative terms often equalled the great principalities – until they fell victim to repeated partitions or the greed of mighty princely neighbours.

Among those lesser nobles the imperial knights, whose ancestors had been bound by their person to serve the emperor, represented another special feature of medieval and early modern Germany because they exercised princely sovereignty in miniature – including, for example, the right of capital jurisdiction – on their family estates.

And, despite the constant danger of being subjected to the territorial princes, about 1500 noble families managed, to a large degree, to retain security and independence within the Empire, mainly by forming regional associations under imperial protection.

Thus the imperial knights in particular, as well as the numerous principalities in general, illustrate one of the main features of the political heritage of medieval German history: the fragmentation of political power. Whereas in Western Europe the evolution of strong monarchies provided the basis for the formation of nation-states, in Central Europe the preponderance of centrifugal tendencies created an equilibrium of multifarious political units within an empire in obvious decline. On the other hand, the concept of empire provided another important historical heirloom and up to the twentieth century German history would be bound to the idea of an empire which, transgressing national boundaries, implied if not hegemony at least the aspiration to leadership and supremacy.

THE LAND AND THE PEOPLE

It is not possible to determine the size of Germany's population in the course of the Middle Ages (i.e. between 600 and 1500), not only because of the lack of reliable statistics before the eighteenth century, but also because of a failure to agree on the appropriate geographical boundaries. Some calculations relate to Germany bounded by the frontiers of 1914, others to those of 1937, and rarely do they include either Austria or those parts of the Empire in the south and the west which had effectively become detached in the course of the later Middle Ages, like Switzerland or the Low Countries. Nevertheless some rough estimates have been given, especially for the later period, based on parish registers, tax rolls, rent books etc., and though estimates concerning absolute figures still vary considerably, at least general trends can be established.

The population of Western Europe increased considerably between 600 and 1000 from around 15 million to 23 million; according to other calculations from 18 million in 650 to 38.5 million in the year 1000. The climax of this general increase was reached between the eleventh and the thirteenth centuries. During this period the number of rural settlements in many regions of Germany more than doubled and around 1300 the population of what was to become the Germany of

1914 has been calculated at 14 million people. But this was followed by a spectacular slump in population during the fourteenth century, so that the corresponding figure for 1450 sank to 8–9 million and it was not until the mid-sixteenth century that the population again reached the level of 1300.

This rupture was mainly due to the plague, which swept over Europe from 1347, when Italian merchant ships brought it from Central Asia. It caused the severest demographic catastrophe ever known in Europe, far worse in its effects than even the Second World War. The first wave of the disease led to the death of at least 25 per cent of the population and it was followed by new outbreaks at relatively short intervals. Such losses are indicated by the number of deserted settlements throughout the regions of Germany where as many as 40,000 out of a total of 170,000 disappeared, either temporarily or permanently.

As in most of Europe, the great mass of the German people, about 90 per cent of the population, were peasants and paupers, living on and from the land, and providing the basis of the social pyramid of medieval society, with the pious priests and the noble warriors at the top. Throughout the Middle Ages – and not only during the years of the plague – the life of the common man was miserable, brutish and short, not only because of the high infant mortality rate but also because of the manifold vicissitudes of a life exposed to recurring famine and nearly continuous warfare.

In Carolingian times it became increasingly difficult for the free warrior to render military service to the king and at the same time to till his lands. This led to a momentous division of labour between the knight and the peasant. And those who had to lay down the sword in favour of the plough soon lost their freedom since they now had to rely on the noble warrior for protection, and he became their lord of the manor. Thus, in the course of time, the great majority of the people became part of a manorial system which provided the basic pattern for medieval agrarian society. In fact, the common man was not the king's subject, but his lord's man, his landlord's serf. He had lost his freedom, was bound to the customs of the manor, subjected to the jurisdiction of the lord, tied to his allotment from which neither he nor his children were allowed to move without the lord's permission.

Of course there were numerous variations of seigneurial domination, according to different regions and different historical periods. During the high Middle Ages the old manorial system began to dissolve. By 1300 most landlords had abandoned direct exploitation of their serfs by making them labour on their estates. Instead, they leased out their lands to tenants for rents. At the same time, seigneurial control through the court of the manor was replaced by communes, often wielding considerable powers of local autonomy and self-government. In the western part of Germany at the end of the Middle Ages a land-owning aristocracy lived mainly from rental income, alongside a peasantry who often even had hereditary tenure. But elsewhere, especially after the crisis in the second half of the fourteenth century, a return to various shades and grades of serfdom is discernible. In many regions of Germany, particularly south and east of the Elbe, lords were progressively eroding the peasants' legal status or even their social and economic position.

This revival of serfdom was partly due to economic pressures which stimulated new forms of domanial economy. It was also an instrument of territorial consolidation in which not only the princes but also ecclesiastical lordships like abbeys or even imperial towns were engaged. It occurred mainly in southern and central regions and proved to be the tinder-box for the great Peasants' War of the early sixteenth century. And whereas hardly any signs of this trend towards a 'second serfdom' are noticeable in the north, in the lands east of the Elbe its consequences endured well into the nineteenth century and created another of those many dividing lines within Germany that are characteristic features and factors of its history. To the old boundary between former Roman settlements and the lands north of the *limes* the Middle Ages added a second, running between the lands in the west and those east of the rivers Elbe and Saale.

This was the result of what has been called the 'medieval colonization of the East', the slow but steady expansion of the German-speaking peoples into Slav territory, mainly in the course of the twelfth and thirteenth centuries. Initially it arose from border conflicts in the Eastern Marches, those frontier regions where powerful princes were extending their realms towards the east, and where new dioceses were founded in the midst of Slav territory. But later the Slav rulers themselves initiated and promoted the immigration of German settlers, farmers as well as artisans. The knights of the Teutonic Order were actually summoned to Prussia by Conrad, Duke of Masovia, to aid him in his attempt to carry the Christian faith into the lands of the Prussian tribes.

It was not a mass movement like the great migrations of the third and fourth centuries, and it was only partly caused by the steep demographic upturn during the high Middle Ages. Around 600,000 settlers moved from the western and northern regions of Germany towards the east between 1100 and 1300, mostly in small groups, to found new villages and towns. With them they brought Western cultural achievements to the thinly populated lands east of the Elbe and Saale, from which new German territories emerged: Brandenburg, Prussia, Mecklenburg, Pomerania and Silesia. Over the course of time the Slavs here were assimilated into the German population; in other regions, further to the east, the new German settlers became Poles, Czechs, Slovaks or Hungarians.

Those who decided to go east, often mustered together by their new lords' special agents, were usually offered land under conditions far better than before, so that from now on they enjoyed freedom of personal status and for the first couple of years could even occupy their lands free of rent. But after the crisis of the fourteenth century with its demographic and economic slump, and the introduction of intensified commercial agriculture in East Elbia, lord–peasant relations underwent a profound transformation in many places. Given the opportunity to produce grain for a European market with England as one of the main customers, landlords reverted to direct exploitation of their land, using servile labour, and progressively eroding not only the peasants' legal status but also their social and economic position. Conditions, of course, varied from place to place and from region to region. But generally speaking, in the east both hereditary subjection of the peasant, whereby the terms of his tenancy automatically passed on to his heirs, and serfdom with its obligatory labour-services, were on the increase at the end of the Middle Ages.

On the whole, the living conditions of the common man were the result of certain developments within the general framework of a European economy dominated by agriculture. Initially the introduction of the three-field system of crop rotation and of the horse-drawn heavy iron plough had marked an agricultural revolution that enabled a peasant's family to increase its productivity by at least 50 per cent. Later, during the high Middle Ages, in Germany as elsewhere in Western Europe, the old subsistence economy was replaced by the first moves towards a market economy. This led to various forms of specialization and innovations concerning the methods and techniques of cultivation. Near the towns, crops such as vegetables, vines or hops were grown for the urban market. A general trend towards the extension of pastoralism is discernible in some regions, while others were marked by the emergence of crops such as cereal as a monoculture or the first stirrings of rural industries like textile production, mining and metallurgy.

These shifts in economic developments encouraged the emergence throughout Germany of diverse economic landscapes connected to one another by trade and traffic and at the same time accessible to their European neighbours. Despite temporary setbacks, especially those caused by the Black Death, during the late Middle Ages the gap between the German economy and that of the Mediterranean region increasingly narrowed.

This was due both to change and progress in the agrarian sector and also to the expansion of trade and the beginnings of manufacturing. Both were connected to the rise and growth of the cities, which were not only the focal points within the network of economic landscapes but were also the workshops of progress, the seed-beds of economic and social modernization. Some places, like Cologne, Trier and Augsburg, had origins that went back to Roman times. Others had grown up more recently at the junction of trading routes where fairs had been regularly held. Most of them were the result of political administration and had been founded by emperors, kings, bishops and princes for economic, political, administrative or military reasons. The first of such cities, for example Freiburg (c. 1120), Lübeck (1143) and Munich (1158), were followed by many others, so that by about 1300 the number of cities and towns had more than quadrupled, until in 1450 it reached a total of about 5000 in Central Europe (including Northern France, Poland and Hungary) with around 3000 on German soil. Thus at the end of the Middle Ages between 20 and 30 per cent of the population in the western and southern regions of the German Empire were townspeople, and even in the east and north they constituted about 15 per cent.

Over 90 per cent of these urban settlements were small with between 200 and 2000 inhabitants, and some tiny towns numbered even less. Only 25 German cities had more than 10,000 inhabitants, for example Nuremberg, Augsburg and Würzburg in the south, Bremen, Hamburg, Lübeck and Magdeburg in the north, Prague and Vienna in the east. And in the west Cologne, with more than 40,000 inhabitants, was the biggest German city throughout the Middle Ages. But there was no metropolis like Paris (for which estimates vary between 70,000 and 200,000), Florence, Venice, Milan or Ghent. In Germany there was neither a political capital nor a single centre of manufacturing industries, finance and commerce. Though the network of towns was more densely woven in the south and west, it stretched over the whole Empire and mirrored, in its own sphere, the diversity and multifariousness of Germany.

Towns formed social units distinct from the surrounding countryside, not only because a significant proportion of their population made their living in non-agricultural occupations but also as the result of their legal status. Initially all towns were under the rule of a spiritual or temporal lord. This was often the bishop, especially in cities like Cologne, Mainz, Augsburg and Trier, which since late Roman times had been the capital of a diocese. More often it was the king or some other prince who had founded the town, and who as its ruler was responsible for administration, legislation and law enforcement. But soon townspeople began to organize themselves as self-governing civic communities, at first generally within the scope granted to them by their lord in the form of special privileges, but also by wresting from him the essentials of jurisdiction and administration.

The special privileges usually granted to travelling merchants, along with charters for market rights granted to weekly or annual fairs, were the seeds from which grew the laws of each city, the *ius civitatis*, a body of privileges, laws and customs by which the town and its inhabitants were governed. At the same time, in most places, government meant self-government, not, of course, according to the rules of modern democracy but according to the hierarchical concepts of the Middle Ages – that is, government by the urban elites. They usually controlled the urban council, a body of a dozen or so members, as a rule elected annually by that minority of the urban population who had been granted the freedom of the city. This council, headed by a mayor, actually governed the city.

Thus towns became very special and very important islands in the sea of medieval feudalism. Protected by often impregnable fortifications they stood out as economic, social and often also political units in their own right. The seigneurial rule of the nobility ended at the foot of the walls of medieval towns. Within the political system of the Empire they formed the counterweight to the dominance of the aristocracy in church and state. In particular the right to their own jurisdiction, even in matters concerning life and death, became the hallmark of the autonomy and independence of German medieval cities.

At the same time they remained part of the feudal Empire, especially where they expanded into small city states which themselves rose to feudal lordship over their own vassals. Those which had been founded on old crown lands and had never acknowledged any lord but the emperor called themselves 'imperial cities'; those which had formerly been Sees and had gained their freedom by ousting their bishops called themselves 'free cities'.

The bulk of the imperial cities lay clustered in regions of southern Germany which had always been 'close to the king'. Sometimes they banded together and formed regional leagues, either in the face of threats to their liberty from monarchs and princes, or to promote common economic aims. The most important of these was the Hanseatic League, a league of cities headed by Lübeck, which dominated the trade of the Baltic and North Atlantic from the thirteenth to the sixteenth century and which had grown out of an association of merchants allied in their common commercial interests.

However, on the whole the German towns did not achieve the political significance of the city-states of Northern Italy such as Milan and others, which finally defeated the political aims of German emperors. And their importance started to wane when they were faced with modernized weapons of war which minimized the protection offered by their fortifications. At the close of the Middle Ages many of them had succumbed to the aspirations of neighbouring princes who were plotting consolidating and enlarging their territories. Only a minority succeeded in saving their status as 'free imperial cities' (and thus as a separate part of the German political nation) when they finally achieved a collective vote of their own in the Imperial Diet.

GERMANY AT THE CLOSE OF THE MIDDLE AGES

The course of medieval history in Central Europe had provided no firm basis for a future German national state. Here there were no clear-cut natural frontiers, but a mixture of diverse lands which even forbade the use of 'Germany' as a mere geographical expression. This Central European region comprised a variety of ethnic, cultural, linguistic, social and political formations. At the same time there was no centre, either political or economic, which could serve as a nucleus for future developments as London did for England or the Île de France for the French nation-state.

Instead, the border regions in the west and south forged vital connections with the dynamic economic and cultural centres of Europe in Italy and France. Thus the flowering of Cologne, Nuremberg and Augsburg was the result of the links those cities had established with Northern France or Northern Italy. Germany was bridging the gap between the West and the East, the South and the North. In the process of this economic and cultural transfer it expanded its own influence into the lands of Eastern Europe. To this Bohemia and its capital Prague bear witness, as well as the trading cities of the Baltic like Danzig (Gdánsk) or Reval (Tallin), which had been developed as merchants' settlements by the Hanseatic League.

This loose and shifting pattern of ethnic, economic and cultural variety was overlaid by another pattern of political diversity. Though the Empire provided the outlines of a general framework, this was far too weak and too uncertain to serve as the foundation for a future nation-state.

Especially after the decline and fall of the Hohenstaufen dynasty, the Empire was weakened to such a degree that for some time it was on the brink of sliding into obscurity. After the death of Frederick II in 1250 decades of internal strife and chaos were ushered in so that none of his feeble successors even managed to be crowned in Rome until Henry VII in 1312. And in the following century there were only two emperors to be crowned by the Pope: Sigismund (1433) and – last of all – Frederick III (1452). But by then coronation as the expression of papal approval had lost much of its glamour and importance. In 1338 the seven electors – in a joint declaration – had already set down as law that anyone who had been elected king (*rex romanorum*) by a majority of votes needed no further confirmation to administer the rights and properties of the Empire.

By this privilege of electing not only the king but also the emperor the seven princely electors proved to be the true victors in the long struggle between Papacy and Empire. Naturally, they strove to perpetuate their gains by securing the elective constitution of the Empire as it was set down in the Golden Bull of 1356. In order to prevent the re-establishment of a strong kingdom they started choosing feeble kings from various dynasties; 14 rulers during the late Middle Ages came from six families, and only once (1378) was a father, Charles IV, succeeded by his son, Wenzel.

At the same time, this marked the beginning of a new development. Some of the elected kings had used their title and office to enlarge and strengthen their family possessions and dynastic power, so that in the fifteenth century imperial politics came to be disputed between three leading families: the Bavarian-based Wittelsbachs; the Luxemburgs, who besides Luxemburg and Brabant in the west acquired vast possessions in eastern Central Europe like Bohemia and Silesia; and the Habsburgs of Austria. And when the royal line of Luxemburg became extinct with the death of Siegmund in 1437, and his son-in-law Albrecht of Habsburg was elected emperor the following year, the elective monarchy in fact turned into a quasi-hereditary monarchy. From now on, with one exception (1742), the imperial crown was always to pass to a member of the Habsburg dynasty until the dissolution of the Empire in 1806.

However, although the unrivalled power of the Habsburg dynasty since the end of the Middle Ages precluded any alternative at imperial elections, it did not lead to a rise in imperial power within the Empire. On the contrary, a gulf was opening up between Empire and Emperor. During the reign of the Luxemburg dynasty, those parts of the Empire owned by the family were already in the border regions and later on those of the Habsburgs extended far beyond the imperial frontiers until, during the reign of Charles V they owned lands 'on which the sun would never set'. The Emperor had outgrown the Empire and began to act as a European power in his own right.

This difference was not restricted to the sphere of political geography. Contemporary political thought generated the formula 'Emperor and Empire' (*Kaiser und Reich*), emphasizing that these were two separate elements of the imperial constitution, that the Empire was more than the realm of the Emperor, that at the same time it had become a corporate body comprising the total of an infinite variety of political units: ecclesiastical states and secular princely territories, free and imperial cities, monasteries and the family estates of imperial knights. Slowly the occasional assemblies of the great vassals of the realm at the king's court developed into an Imperial Diet, which in the course of the fifteenth century became the central representative institution of the Empire, consisting of three colleges: electors, princes and cities.

At the same time, from the late fifteenth century the Empire – though there was never an official title – began to be called: 'Holy Roman Empire of the German Nation' (*Heiliges Römisches Reich Deutscher Nation*). This term still stresses continuity, linking it to the Roman Empire as well as to the Christian vision of history as the history of general salvation. But it also now focuses on the heartlands of this empire, and their people (most of whom speak a common language) have German as their native tongue. And because this German Empire began to develop common political institutions like the Diet, where representatives of the German political elites – who made up the nation – established contacts with one another and a rudimentary sense of community started to grow, the late Middle Ages mark the dawn of a German nation.

However, this Empire did not serve as a starting point or even a framework for a German nation-state similar to those taking shape in Western Europe. Instead, the beginnings of the modern state in Central Europe should be traced to the formation of the princely territorial state. Because the princes had to fill the gap left by the weakness of imperial power, in some places they managed to turn feudal power into princely rule over lands and people. At the end of the fifteenth century a number of substantial princely states had established themselves among the welter of petty political rivalries as the leading political forces within the Empire. Among these were the secular electorates of Bohemia, Brandenburg, Saxony and the Rhine Palatinate, as well as major principalities such as Austria, Bavaria, Württemberg and Hesse. They formed the third element in the political heritage of the Middle Ages which, along with Emperor and Empire, was to shape the future course of German history.

3

From the Reformation to the Thirty Years' War

THE EMERGENCE OF THE MODERN AGE

At the turn of the fifteenth century, quite a number of outstanding events marked the dawn of a new age, the beginning of the period of modern European history:

* In 1453 Constantinople, the capital of the Byzantine Empire, was taken by the Ottoman Turks, which brought the long history of the Eastern Roman Empire to an end. In the wake of this catastrophe many Greek scholars migrated to Italy, thus effecting a huge transfer of the spiritual heritage of classic antiquity to Europe, which gave a monumental boost to the Renaissance movement.
* In 1492, in search of a new route to the riches of the Far East, Columbus 'discovered' America. From now on Europe began to conquer the rest of the world – this marks the beginning of the process of globalization.
* In 1494, King Charles VIII of France invaded Italy and conquered the Kingdom of Naples, an event which is often regarded as the starting point not only of the conflict between France and the Habsburg Empire, which was to last for more than two centuries, but of modern power politics.
* In 1517, the Saxon monk Martin Luther published 95 'theses' directed against the practice of the Church selling indulgences. With this he set off a chain of actions and reactions, finally leading to the break-up of the unity of Christendom which had been the dominant feature of the European Middle Ages.

Moreover, these events have to be set against a background made up of certain general trends and developments, such as:

- the rise of modern capitalism in the field of economics;
- the formation of the early modern state as the focal point of the concentration of power in human society;
- the emergence of a public sphere following the invention of printing;
- the general intellectual change brought about by the Renaissance, i.e. the rediscovery of antique traditions in the field of arts and letters.

All those events and trends affected the course of German history to varying degrees. The expansion of the Ottoman power soon became a major threat to the Empire – in 1529 a Turkish army for the first time laid siege to Vienna. Although Emperor Charles V was King of Spain and therefore ruler of vast possessions overseas, Germany did not profit directly and immediately from the new riches – on the contrary, old trade centres like Lübeck suffered from the general shift of the main trading routes to ports at the Atlantic coast. At the same time Charles V was the main antagonist of French expansion to Italy and thus the German Empire again and again became involved in this new game of European power-politics and was even turned into its central battlefield. And whereas in Western Europe, in England, Spain and France, the formation of the modern state took place on the grand scale of new national monarchies, in Germany only comparably small principalities led the way to political modernization.

However, the Reformation, which brought about the end of the unity of the Western European Church, and the end of the undisputed spiritual leadership of the Pope by division of Latin Christendom into Protestants and Catholics, was of German origin. And thus it became one of the decisive factors in the course of German history.

This singular event sprang from a multiplicity of causes. First of all, there was the general decline of the European Church since the stunning victory of the Papacy over the emperors in the thirteenth century. In 1302, Pope Boniface VIII in his bull *Unam Sanctam* had unreservedly proclaimed the world supremacy of the Papacy, but only seven years later the popes became prisoners of the French kings in Avignon for more than half a century. And immediately afterwards the Great Schism, which lasted from 1378 to 1417, divided Europe into the camps of the supporters of two – and in the end of even three – rival popes.

When the schism was finally resolved by the Council of Constance (1414–18) and only a short time later the Council of Basle (1431–49) began to tackle the huge task of a general reform of the Church, a new conflict arose: whether those general councils of the Church should meet regularly and even establish their supremacy over the Pope. And even though this conciliar movement was defeated in the end and declared a heresy, it was to haunt the Papacy throughout the century before the Reformation.

Besides internal strife the general authority of the Church was further damaged by the ascending new national monarchies in the West. Their rulers made use first of the schism and then of the conflict at the Council of Basle to bargain successfully for more or less 'national churches' as, for example, Charles VII did for France, when in 1439 he issued the *Pragmatic Sanction of Bourges* to curtail the Pope's right to appoint candidates to French church offices: the powers of the secular state were on the advance.

PRE-REFORMATION GERMANY

In Germany the position of the Church was more complex than elsewhere, because there was no unequalled sovereign as in France or England to extract conditions from the Papacy. Here, in Germany, some princes – among them the rulers of Bavaria, Saxony, Austria and Brandenburg – managed to tighten their grip on ecclesiastical rights and benefices, so that the Duke of Cleves is reported to have claimed that he was pope in his own lands. But on the other hand there still existed many intrusions by the papal bureaucracy into the revenues of the German Church. Those clerics who had been appointed to their offices or livings by the Pope had to transfer part of their first year's annuities to Rome; ecclesiastical jurisdiction was another source of income, as were dispensations and licences requested to evade the terms of canon law.

All this became a cause for growing resentment, especially as the Pope was soon regarded not only as the head of a universal Church, but also as a foreign power. On the one hand, this resentment was due to the fact that during the fifteenth century the policy of the See of Rome more and more began to aim at the foundation and extension of a Papal State in central Italy and some popes even strove to found dynasties; on the other hand, this criticism was also due to the first stirrings of nationalism in Europe.

Even in Germany Renaissance humanism was tinged with a new intellectual patriotism. Though the origins of the German movement were, as elsewhere, closely linked to the rediscovery of classical antiquity by Italian scholars, German intellectuals soon started to look for their own roots, which they found in 'Germania', the lands north of the Danube and east of the Rhine, as they had been described by the Roman historian Tacitus in his book *Germania* which had been published in Italy again in 1455. Thus German humanists like the Alsatian scholar Jacob Wimpfeling found their ancestors as equals to the Greeks and Romans and to the ancient Franks or Anglo-Saxons. At the turn of the century among the intellectual elite of the Empire the foundations of a German national consciousness were laid which could now be linked to a new national myth. And as Tacitus in his time (about AD 100) had praised the moral integrity of the ancient Germanic people in order to hold up a mirror to his contemporaries, whom he thought flawed by debauchery and corruption, so now German humanists set the unspoilt morals of their countrymen against the base licentiousness of the Italians, especially of the members of the Papal Court in Rome, who at the same time were seen to act as a continuous drain on the financial resources of Germany. This was one of the main public grievances, the 'gravamina nationis germanicae' put forward by the Estates of the Diet of the Empire (i.e. the political nation) in 1456 and again and again in numerous pamphlets. So when Luther complained in 1520 of 'such a swarm of parasites in that place called Rome . . . lying in wait for the endowments and benefices of Germany as wolves lie in wait for the sheep' he was only echoing long-standing sentiments.[1]

Thus a new, national dimension was added to the general criticism of the Church that had been voiced in most of the European countries in the late Middle Ages, attacking the abuse of the spiritual privileges of the Church, the excessive growth of its bureaucracy, and the dubious qualities of priests and preachers.

But anti-clericalism, though doubtlessly vigorous and growing, did not in itself present a mortal danger to the Church. For in spite of the obvious dawn of a new age, Christian religion was still governing men's minds and souls. Where life for most people was miserable, brutish and short, because its essentials were beyond their control and foresight, the prospect of another, eternal, life after death offered singular consolation. Heaven was the goal everyone strove to attain and the Church of Rome still kept the key to its gate. And though religious belief of the masses remained interspersed with 'superstition', with the many relics of ancient popular cults and rites, everyone knew that his salvation in the end depended upon the powers of the Church. For since the fall of Adam and Eve man was prone to sin and could only be redeemed by the aid of the Church, whose dogma contained the means necessary to overcome the despair of the sinner.

And despite much criticism this primary function, this essential religious monopoly of the Church, was not contested. On the contrary, all over Europe, the fifteenth century was an age of rising popular piety. Growing numbers of pilgrims took part in more and more pilgrimages, the number of religious feasts and pageants increased, and there was an increasing demand for books of prayer and images of the saints. On the whole, lay devotion to a conventional, ritualized piety was increasing and thus the means of grace and salvation offered by the Church continued to be in constant demand.

On the eve of the Reformation, the Church was by no means in decay but in quite a strong position. It had successfully overcome the dangers of the schism and the challenge of the conciliar movement and its claims in matters of dogma were generally accepted without dispute, as was the concept of a unique Church. But to the same extent as popular piety was on the increase, the shortcomings and deficiencies of the Church as an institution and of its personnel were becoming more and more evident and the object of growing general criticism, which in the end resulted in widespread anti-clericalism, not only in Germany. This paradoxical situation led to a precarious equilibrium: as long as the Church represented the only way to salvation for the vast majority of the people, its position was more or less unassailable. But as soon as someone like Martin Luther offered a convincing alternative this precarious balance could be tipped and criticism of the Church could turn into a fundamental religious transformation of European society.

LUTHER'S REBELLION

The Reformation was more than the climax of the crisis of the Church of Christ at the end of the fifteenth century, for again and again this church had successfully dealt with crises, the last time with the Hussite movement in Bohemia (which to a certain extent had anticipated the Protestant Reformation, but had been contained and finally defeated, because it had been an essentially Czech phenomenon). Instead, the outbreak and the effects of the Reformation cannot be separated from the person of Martin Luther. And though the Reformation was also a series of parallel movements – within which different leaders like Thomas Cromwell in England and Jean Calvin in Geneva pursued different objects – it began with Luther, when in autumn 1517 he fixed 95 'theses' for an academic disputation on the power of indulgences to the door of the castle church in the small Saxon university town of Wittenberg.

Born in 1483, Martin Luther had joined the mendicant order of the Augustinian Eremites in 1505, took his degree in theology in 1512 and then was given a chair for biblical studies at the University of Wittenberg. During all those years he had suffered from his tender conscience, from the conviction of his own shortcomings as a vessel of sin and from the uncertainty of his salvation. This very personal anguish of his soul provided the driving force of his studies which, in the end, led to revolutionary results. Though he was a formidable intellect, Luther was not like the modern intellectual who criticizes and attacks religion from a detatched position. Instead, Luther's problem was the central concern of medieval man: how to achieve salvation in the face of man's sinfulness by the grace of God who, at the same time, is meting out stern divine justice. He finally found his solution in St Paul's Letters to the Romans I:17, where it says that man's salvation is founded solely on his belief in God's mercy.

In itself, such a tenet – though a frontal assault on scholastic theology – was not a heresy and Luther considered it merely as a challenge in the context of academic disputation. And when published, it evoked no response whatever. But the bombshell exploded when, in his capacity as a priest, he turned against the selling of letters of indulgence by members of the rival order of the Dominican Friars. According to established usage, the sinner regained the state of grace by confession, followed by priestly absolution for which he had to perform a work of satisfaction, commonly called 'penance'. This penance could be cancelled out by an 'indulgence' offered by the Church, which was based on the belief that the Church held a huge store of surplus merit accumulated by Christ, the Virgin and the Saints, which it now could assign to whom it chose, that is, to any who purchased it for a certain price. For the Church this meant an additional source of income to finance certain projects like crusades or, in this case, the building of St Peter's in Rome.

Thus Luther's challenge provoked vigorous reaction not only on the part of the Dominican Order but from the established church as a whole. In the course of the ensuing war of pamphlets and public disputations Luther saw himself goaded on to a wholesale attack on the monopoly of the means of grace that the Church claimed to possess by his re-examination of the traditional theology of salvation. Finally, Luther reached the conclusion that St Paul's words, 'The just shall live by faith' (Romans I:17), implied the fundamental rejection of the belief that salvation comes through grace received in the sacraments and other rites of the traditional Church. Instead, when, according to Luther's famous insight, justification is achieved through faith alone, the Church becomes the community of the faithful, the aggregate of all those Christians who truly believe. And when Luther had to defend his position against traditional concepts of authority put forward by the papalist school, he had to find a source of authority more credible and more venerable than the institutional Church. He and his followers found that in the authority of 'the Word'. And as Christ was the sole mediator between Man and God, the Scripture was the sole authority for Christ's message.

The first climax in this conflict was reached when Luther was found guilty of heresy and on 15 June 1520 a papal bull condemned him and 41 tenets drawn from his works, allowing him 60 days to recant or to face excommunication. Then the Pope joined forces with Emperor Charles V. Luther was summoned to the *Reichstag* – the general assembly of the estates of the empire – and again asked to recant. But again Luther answered: 'Unless I am convinced by the testimony of the Scripture . . . I neither can nor will revoke anything!'[2]

One year later, Luther had been excommunicated by the Church, placed under ban in the Holy Roman Empire, and cited as a heretic by Rome's leading theologians. But at the same time, what had started as a very personal matter between one monk and his church had expanded into a movement which overwhelmed not only Germany but most of Europe. 'All of Germany is in open revolt. Nine tenth cry out "Luther"! And as for the remaining tenth, in so far as they are not bothered about Luther, they see the solution in the slogan "Death to the Roman court" ', the papal nuncio reported back to the papal court from Germany as early as 1521.

Reformers of all stamps and nationalities raised their voices; the most influential among them were Huldrych Zwingli and Jean Calvin in Switzerland, which became the second source for the dissemination of the Protestant creed. And of course, as with every revolutionary movement, there was a radical fringe: Anabaptists made their appearance in Saxony, challenging not only the traditional Church but the established political order as well, seeking to found an ideal Christian republic. This Christian fundamentalism fought for a radical realization of the message of the Gospel – even at the cost of violence – and it was roundly condemned by Luther. At the same time, outbursts of social unrest could easily be linked to the message of the Reformation. When members of the petty nobility, knights of the Empire, rose in a futile effort against the advance of the princely territorial state (1522–3), prominent members like Ulrich von Hutten and Franz von Sickingen had also supported Luther's message.

Far more serious was the 'Peasants' War' (1524–5), the last in a number of outbursts of violent rebellion by the rural population at the close of the Middle Ages. They arose basically from economic and legal grievances and in their final and most violent stage, the rebels, with their 'twelve articles', proclaimed elaborate and sweeping plans for social reform before their rebellion was crushed with the utmost brutality. They had tried to link their defiance of political authority to the way Luther had defied the authority of the Church. But when the leaders asked Luther for his judgement on their articles, he proved himself a staunch defender of the social order with the publication of his trenchant appeal *Against the Murderous and Thieving Hordes of Peasants*.

THE DYNAMICS OF THE REFORMATION

The manifold and far-reaching impact the Reformation had on the course of European history in general and German history in particular leads to the obvious question of *how* it was effected, how the Reformation interacted with the trends and tensions of the period and how its doctrine was transformed into the social and cultural reality of the Protestant Churches.

In view of his perseverance and his determination neither to recant nor water down any of his tenets by compromise, Luther might well have shared the fate of all those who at various times had been declared heretics by the Church and burnt at the stake. But from the beginning allies from different camps rallied around him, ready to support his case or help protect him against persecution by his enemies. There were German humanists like Philipp Melanchthon and Ulrich von Hutten, artists like Albrecht Dürer and Lukas Cranach, and above all, numerous eminent members of the clergy like Martin Bucer in Strasbourg and Andreas Osiander in Nuremberg, ready and eager to spread the new gospel. Even more important was support from the sphere of high politics: when Luther left the Diet of Worms in April 1521, soon to be outlawed, Frederick 'the Wise', the Elector of Saxony, had him abducted and secretly taken into protective custody in his castle of Wartburg, where Luther soon began to translate the New Testament into German.

However, the success of the Reformation was mainly due to the widespread support it gained in the public sphere, not only among those who might be called the members of the 'political nation', that is, persons or groups of persons of means and influence who could write and read, but also among a wider public, the masses of the church-going population. The speed with which the new gospel spread was also of fundamental importance. Not only did Luther write pamphlets at an astonishing rate (in 1520, for example, he wrote 27), they were published almost immediately and achieved a large circulation; between 1518 and 1520 there were 20 editions of his *Sermon on Indulgence and Grace*, and his address *To the Christian Nobility of the German Nation* sold 4000 copies within 18 days, and just one week after its publication the second edition had been printed. This was mainly due to the fact that most of the time he wrote not in Latin, addressing his learned colleagues, but in German, in order to reach the common man. Already in 1518 the first edition of his complete works had appeared and at the time of the Diet of Worms more than 500,000 copies of his books and pamphlets had been sold; this figure rose to several millions in 1525.

And Luther – though he might for some years have been the author of a third of the total of all new publications in German – was not the only one; there were others as well, arguing for or against his gospel. Thus in the year 1524 2.4 million copies of 2400 different pamphlets were published. Obviously, the success of the Reformation depended at least partly on a media revolution, made possible by the invention of printing. But the printed letter reached only the small minority of those able to read. More could be influenced by printed pictures – woodcuttings for example – which were employed as the means of a new kind of pictorial propaganda. But most were converted to the new gospel by the power of the spoken word, by those preaching this gospel.

This underlines the fact that the Reformation in its first stage was mainly an urban event. The urban setting provided the conditions favourable for the reception and dissemination of its ideas. Here the reformers first held their sermons and published their pamphlets; public life was civic life. And the urban culture of communality proved especially receptive to the new Protestant Church, which was based on the idea of the congregation as a community of the faithful. In 1535 there remained only a handful of substantial cities – like Cologne, Würzburg, Bamberg and Freiburg im Breisgau – where the reform movement had either failed or been suppressed.

However, to survive and, what is more, to create its own establishment and organization in the face of a Catholic Church soon determined to regain lost ground and an emperor who aspired to rebuild the unity of the Holy Christian Empire, Protestantism needed a more powerful political stronghold than the cities could provide. This was achieved by the alliance with the agents of political modernization – when the new creed merged with the political aims of territorial sovereigns in German principalities and European kingdoms.

In a second stage in Germany, the Reformation as an evangelical mass movement was replaced by the political move of a number of princely estates of the Empire. And though this may have been based on the personal conversion of some rulers, it was also the case that the new Protestantism offered new opportunities for those rulers to expand their power and to establish their sovereignty. Because of the separation from Rome, the new churches needed their own administrative framework; and this is where the Protestant magistrates stepped in. They took over the function of the former bishops, replaced the former diocesan officials by new superintendents and organized church visitations.

Though this had never been intended by Luther and his fellow reformers, in effect the Church became an organ of state governance, since the Diet of Speyer (1526) had resolved that control over religious matters should be left to individual sovereign bodies within the Empire. An unprecedented fusion of Church and state took place, not only in the realm of administration, but also because confessional unity was regarded as the basis for political stability and a reinforcement of national or territorial identity. Moreover, control over the Church also meant control over church property as an important additional instrument of power.

In the course of the sixteenth century nearly the whole of Europe was affected by the Reformation as it spread rapidly from its sources in Germany and Switzerland. Only Spain and Italy remained strongholds of the Roman Catholic Church. The religious politics of the Empire were delicately balanced. Though most emperors were determined to suppress the new gospel for the sake of religious conformity within the Empire, the other three lay electors were Protestants as were most of the German princely territories by the middle of the century. Of major Catholic powers, only Bavaria and Austria were left alongside the numerous remaining prince-bishoprics and great abbey estates. In the second half of the century the expansion of Protestantism had reached its climax in Germany.

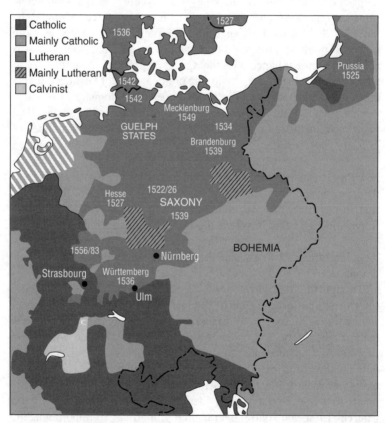

Map 2 Reformation Germany (adapted from Hagen Schulze, *Kleine deutsche Geschichte mit Bildern aus dem Deutschen Historischen Museum* (Munich, 1996), p. 50).

CONFESSIONALIZATION

After the Pope and his Church had been on the defensive for some time, they then started to turn the tables. A thorough reform of the church was achieved by the Council of Trent (1545–63), which provided the doctrinal definitions and institutional structures that enabled the Roman Church not only to withstand the Protestant challenge but to initiate an offensive which marked the beginning of a Counter-Reformation. Traditional views and doctrines were reaffirmed against the various Protestant alternatives. At the same time the authority of the Pope was strengthened, conformity and church discipline were not only enforced but also openly displayed. The impact of this Catholic reform was soon felt right across Europe. In the Emperor's Austrian lands it formed a close alliance with the dynasty and its politics and elsewhere in Germany the balance between Catholics and Protestants became even more uneasy.

For in the meantime all chances for reuniting the different camps of the Christian faith had vanished into thin air. To the same extent as Catholicism had reaffirmed its traditional doctrines, the different branches of Protestantism had defined the tenets of their creed. Luther's followers at the Diet of Augsburg in 1530 presented a summary of their beliefs, composed by Melanchthon – the so-called 'Confession of Augsburg' – as the official Protestant manifesto. And though this had defined their position as closely as possible within the Church's tradition, the Catholic majority regarded it as a heretical document. However, from now on there existed not only this gulf between the traditional and the new creed – obviously not to be closed or even bridged – but soon new fissures appeared within the Protestant camp, between Lutherans and the followers of Zwingli and Calvin.

Doctrinally they all shared Luther's belief in the absolute authority of the Bible and in justification of the sinner by faith alone. But they differed on other matters, such as on the nature of the Holy Communion which, after the abolition of the Catholic Mass, became the focal point of Protestant worship; on forms of church organization; as well as on the political implications of their spiritual message. Three decades after the formulation of the Augsburg Confession the 'Heidelberg Catechism', issued in 1563, became the main confessional statement of the Calvinists.

Thus after the middle of the sixteenth century, detailed and explicit confessions (that is, statements of faith) set out the essentials of the different Christian doctrines. These were at the centre of what German historians have recently characterized as 'confessionalization' – a process which 'enabled the spirit of confessional Christianity to penetrate, transform and then reform the state, culture, the legal and intellectual realm, and indeed society' as a whole.[3] In spite of many and various forms of revolutionary change, religion had not become just a private matter; on the contrary, religious beliefs were even more than before a matter of public concern and formed a constituent part of national political identity within the framework of the evolving modern states.

THE IMPACT OF THE REFORMATION ON THE COURSE OF GERMAN HISTORY

In considering the manifold far-reaching effects of the Reformation on the course of German history, the historian will come to paradoxical conclusions. In his own time Luther was regarded by many German humanist scholars as a national hero and later German national mythology saw him in the tradition of Arminius, venerating him as one of the founding fathers of the German nation. In actual fact, however, Luther's Reformation produced profound and long-lasting religious, political and cultural divides within the nascent German nation.

Whereas in Western Europe, as soon as confessional conformity had been established – though often as the result of prolonged and bloody inner wars as in France – powerful nation-states were on the advance, the merely partial success of the Reformation in Germany stood in the way of further political and cultural integration. And though at the turn of the century various projects had been discussed and even efforts made to reorganize the constitution of the Empire in order to strengthen its efficiency, the Reformation effected further consolidation of the self-sufficiency of the territorial states. As a minority in the councils of the estates of the Empire, the Protestant rulers had to be watchful guardians of their liberties against the efforts of the emperor and his Catholic allies to restore religious unity. Thus the Reformation intensified the centrifugal tendencies within the loose framework of the Empire.

On the other hand, it contributed to the extension of the power of the state by eliminating the old Church as its autonomous rival, putting its resources at the disposal of the government, which at the same time extended its control over its subjects by supervising and controlling the new Church. The position of the state was further strengthened by Luther's doctrine of political obedience, which he had clearly stated in the early 1520s when he saw his teachings perverted by radical Anabaptists and rebellious peasants. He insisted that secular authorities rule by the ordinance of God and that it was the subject's duty to obey, no matter how imperfect those rulers might be.

Thus, in a twofold manner the Reformation stood in the way of the formation of a German nation-state: it not only reinforced political fragmentation but also added a new religious divide with both political and general cultural implications, constituting an active factor of German history up to the present day.

Though Luther's translation of the Bible, which soon became the most widely read book in Germany, contributed decisively to the formation and expansion of a more or less uniform German language (which soon served as a solid basis for the evolution of a German nation as a cultural unit), there still existed distinct frontiers between Catholic and Protestant culture following the ancient border which had separated the zone of Roman influence from the lands of the Germanic tribes. For Catholicism possessed its strongholds in the south and west of the Empire, though with the exception of most of the larger cities. Here, in the wake of the Counter-Reformation and strongly influenced by Italian and French artists, the splendours of the baroque were displayed in the capitals and courts of the numerous ecclesiastical and secular rulers, where the fine arts were cultivated.

In the northern and eastern parts of Central Europe, where Protestantism dominated, an austere intellectual climate prevailed. As Luther had stressed the importance of the written word, the Bible, literacy spread faster than elsewhere, governments paid more attention to the field of education, to schools and universities; here the ground was prepared for the reception and discussion of the results of the 'Scientific Revolution' of the age of Copernicus, Bacon and Galileo. And while in the Catholic south opera and theatre flourished, in the north with the new Lutheran order of worship church music played a prominent role in turning Germany into the most musically educated nation in Europe. The genius of Bach could have found no better soil than in Lutheranism.

Thus, with the general consequences of the Reformation, diversity in many respects became even more the trademark of Germany and its history.

THE AGE OF THE WARS OF RELIGION

The break-up of the unity of the Western European Church had resulted in a number of competing churches, each trying to define their tenets as precisely as possible and thereby to distinguish themselves from their rivals. This resulted in growing rigidity of religious attitudes influencing all aspects of social, cultural and political life. And when at the same time the secular rulers not only extended their influence in the sphere of ecclesiastical matters but also tried to impose a uniform faith on their subjects in order to achieve and strengthen political conformity, the consequence was the challenge of permanent confessional conflict. The age of the Reformation was followed by the age of the Wars of Religion.

But while France was rent by religious warfare between Catholics and Protestant Huguenots during the second half of the sixteenth century, Germany at first successfully escaped such disasters. Though the Reformation had failed to gain total victory within the Empire, so that here both confessions were engaged in a struggle for supremacy, open armed conflict was avoided for the time being; religious tensions could, to a certain extent, be defused. This was due to the political structure of the Empire. The authority and power of the Emperor did not extend far enough to enable him to enforce religious uniformity. And even though Charles V and his successors were bent on restoring the supremacy of Catholicism, the *de facto* power of the territorial rulers led to a kind of co-existence of the different confessions within the Empire.

This principle had been proclaimed for the first time by the Recess Declaration of the Diet of Speyer (1526), where the Protestant opponents of the Emperor had succeeded in inserting the formula for princely liberty in the matters of religion. And though with the growing impact of the Counter-Reformation Catholicism started regaining lost ground in Germany, the precarious equilibrium between the confessions could be maintained throughout the second half of the century. The guidelines for a way to some kind of religious toleration within the Empire had been defined by the 'Peace of Augsburg' at the Diet of Augsburg in 1555. First it set down that two religions could legally be practised: Roman Catholicism and Lutheranism as defined by the *confessio Augustana* of 1530. It then provided, in essence, for the princes and the other estates of the Empire to choose one of these confessions for themselves and their subjects – a prerogative which was later summarized in the maxim '*cuius regio, eius religio*'.

This prerogative of the rulers flowed from their *ius reformandi*, their right to reform and organize the Church within their territory. Their subjects, on the other hand, by no means enjoyed freedom of conscience but had either to accept the religious predilections of their master or to emigrate – a dubious privilege in the light of actual living conditions for the great majority of the common people. Only in some of the imperial cities was genuine religious toleration – i.e. equal rights for both confessions – guaranteed.

And important questions still remained unresolved, which would soon become matters of dispute. In order to bar the further advance of the Reformation, the Catholic estates had added a further clause which forbade the *ius reformandi* for ecclesiastical princes who decided to convert to Protestantism. Instead, they were asked to resign to ensure the survival of the Catholic ecclesiastical principalities. The Protestants never consented to this clause. Moreover, the Calvinist Protestant denomination was not even mentioned in the treaty though the Empire was *de facto* tri-confessional – up to 1600, in principalities like the Electoral Palatinate, Hesse-Kassel, Cleves, Berg and Jülich, Calvinistic Church structures and forms had been adopted because their rulers had converted to the tenets of Calvinism.

In fact, the 'Peace' of Augsburg was nothing more than a truce that shelved only temporarily the outbreak of open conflict between Catholics and Protestants, as neither side was sincere when agreeing to the compromise of 1555. The ardent religious fervour which had provided the momentum for the formation of the different confessions did not allow genuine toleration. On the contrary: both sides still aimed at total victory, and concessions made to the other side were regarded as no more than a temporary expedient. At the same time, there is no denying that in the wake of the Peace of Augsburg Germany experienced the longest stretch of peace in its history up to the present time: apart from one minor disturbance it lasted for 63 years; the conflict was building up slowly but steadily.

A gradual change in the uneasy *modus vivendi* between Catholics and Protestants was brought about by the growing self-confidence of the party of the Counter-Reformation. In alliance with the Emperor they slowly began to bring to bear the structural majority they enjoyed in the councils, courts and committees of the Empire. The Protestants began to feel that the statutes of the Empire which had granted them protection could no longer be relied on. Therefore, under the leadership of the Elector Palatine those Protestant towns and princes which felt most threatened in 1608 formed the *Union* as a defensive confessional alliance. The Catholics reacted by founding the *Liga* in the following year. Now two war-camps had been formed and from 1608 on several occasions the Empire found itself on the brink of open armed conflict.

THE THIRTY YEARS' WAR

Ten years later war broke out and right from the beginning it was more than just a religious struggle. When on 23 May 1618 the delegates of the Bohemian Protestants threw the two regents of the absent King and Emperor out of the window of the council chamber in Prague, they started a revolt against the policy of their Catholic ruler and his allies to undermine the rights of the Protestants in the kingdom. But soon this revolt accelerated into a constitutional struggle aiming at the establishment of the supremacy of the Protestant estates in Bohemia which, indeed, in the following year passed a resolution to depose the future emperor Ferdinand as their king. And when they elected Frederick, the Calvinist Elector Palatine and head of the Protestant Union instead, the rebellion turned into war on a large scale.

But after he had been elected emperor in 1619, Ferdinand II formed an alliance with the Catholic *Liga* and struck back. As the members of the Protestant Union wavered in their support for the Bohemian rebels, the latter were crushed at the great battle of the White Mountain in November 1620 and Bohemia and Moravia were subjected to a savage campaign of repression. Then war was carried into the lands of the defeated Elector Palatine and afterwards the Catholic armies turned north, because the Emperor and the *Liga* intended to reap the harvest of their military supremacy by trying to regain all those former ecclesiastical lands which had been lost to the Reformation since 1552.

After a series of further sweeping victories against Protestant princes and even their formidable ally, the King of Denmark, this policy was reaffirmed and made explicit by the Emperor's *Edict of Restitution* of 1629. This marked the climax of imperial power – for the last time in German history the Emperor was close to asserting his domination over the estates of the Empire, of re-establishing confessional uniformity within the Empire by crushing the heresy of Protestantism, and of securing the supremacy of the Habsburg dynasty as the leading European power.

But it was as a result of this victory that in fact 1629 marked the turning point of the war, especially its final extension and transition into a general European conflict. Spain as the Habsburg twin power had been involved from the beginning and even more so when its war with the United Provinces of the Netherlands was resumed in 1621. In 1628 Gustavus Adolphus, King of Sweden, entered the lists, not only as the defender of endangered Protestantism but also because he was concerned as to the impact the imperial power, which now extended to the German coastline of the Baltic, might have on Swedish interests in this area. He was supported by France, which since the beginning of the sixteenth century had fought to break the encirclement by the expanding Habsburg power stretching from the Netherlands to Spain. It finally formally declared war on the German Emperor and Spain in 1635 and, although having subdued the Protestant Huguenots at home, became an ally of the Protestant camp on the German scene. And because of the rising number of participants ensnared in a network of shaky alliances it became more and more difficult to reach a final peace settlement. Some historians have distinguished at least 13 different wars and ten different peace treaties within the span between 1618 and 1648. And even after 1648 war between France and Spain dragged on until the final victory of the French in 1659.

Thus religious and constitutional conflict in Bohemia had finally mushroomed into a huge European war with Germany as its main battlefield. And in this theatre of war great actors entered the stage and memorable battle scenes were produced: the general of the army of the Catholic *Liga*, Count Tilly, the victor of Prague who later – to the horror of the Protestant world – stormed, sacked and burnt down Magdeburg, where about 20,000 men and women lost their lives. Only four months later, in September 1631, his army of 31,000 men was routed in one of the greatest battles of the entire war by 41,000 Protestants under the command of the King of Sweden, Gustavus Adolphus. He became the shining hero of the Protestant cause, the more so, as only one year later he met his death in the indecisive battle of Lützen, where, after the Swedes had been able to hold the battlefield, his naked body was discovered under a heap of fallen soldiers. The commanding general on the other side was Albrecht von Wallenstein, the great but enigmatic imperial warlord, who had twice been able to gather huge armies of his own and put them at the disposal of the Emperor. But when his success and power grew and he started to develop and pursue his own political aims, he was murdered at the Emperor's command.

Yet, none of the great battles was decisive enough to end the fighting and to allow the victor to dictate the terms of peace, so the war
dragged on with its gruesome reality of daily hardships for the people
of Germany. This meant pillage and plunder, and often rape and
murder, and as a rule famine and diseases as the consequences of
extreme dearth and poverty. For the huge armies had to live off the
land and its people.

Wallenstein's success largely depended on his ability to make 'the
war feed the war' by developing to an unprecedented degree the
system of extorting contributions from occupied provinces. And
though there were some regions, especially in the north-west, which
had hardly been touched by the war, in the end Germany lay desolate
– the population had shrunk from 17 to 10 million. Some districts were
depopulated, some cities like Magdeburg stood in ruins, trade had
virtually ceased. And it was the lower orders of society, mainly in the
rural districts – and here the old and the very young – who were most
affected by the consequences of the war. But neither was being a
soldier a safe bet. On the average, annual losses of around 30 per cent
for every military unit of soldiers seems to have been the normal
quota, again not so much caused by military action as by typhoid,
plague and other diseases.

THE PEACE OF WESTPHALIA

As the war was long, peace took a long time in coming; even the final
rounds of general negotiations dragged on for more than three years.
In June 1645 the envoys of the Crowns of France and Sweden
presented their propositions for peace in Münster (venue for the
Catholic side) and Osnabrück (venue for the Protestant side). And as
not only the Emperor, but all estates and princes of the Empire had
been invited, negotiations comprised not only an international peace
conference but at the same time an Imperial Diet.

When finally the copious document of the Peace of Westphalia was
signed on 24 October 1648, three fundamental issues had been settled.
The first was the religious strife in Germany between the rival confessions. From now on the same rights were granted to the Reformed
Protestants (the Calvinists) as to Catholics and Lutherans. For the
settling of all religious conflicts over church properties and confessional allegiance it was agreed to accept the status of the year 1624 as

48

the norm for the resolution of all disputes. And in future, confessional disputes within the Empire were no longer to be solved by majority decisions, but by negotiations between the Catholic and Protestant estates, who, from now on, would act as separate bodies as far as questions of religion were concerned. It had taken 30 years of warfare to more or less confirm the confessional status quo that had been reached in the middle of the previous century.

On the constitutional issue, which had loomed large especially in the 1620s when the Emperor had threatened to regain supremacy, the 'Liberties of the Estates' were declared inviolate. This meant that the near-sovereignty of the princes was reaffirmed. Moreover, they were now granted the right to sign treaties with foreign powers, and all imperial legislation as well as all major political decisions concerning the Empire were made conditional on the Diet's approval. The political balance in Germany was finally changed in favour of the political autonomy of individual princes at the expense of the power of the Emperor.

This went together with the settlement on the third fundamental issue, the European issue. Here France had intended to destroy the Habsburg influence in Central Europe and this was now partly achieved by substantial territorial gains in the western border region of the Empire. It thereby controlled the lines of support for the Spanish armies in the Netherlands, so that Spain, which had not joined the negotiations, was finally forced to acknowledge the independence of the Dutch Republic. At the same time Sweden acquired important footholds on the German coast of the Baltic and the North Sea with the mouths of the rivers Elbe, Weser and Oder. Thus the Treaty marked the beginning of the end of Habsburg hegemony over Europe, only to be replaced by French supremacy.

Actual peace took a long time to be felt (the last Swedish troops did not leave until 1654). But it was greeted by the people who had lived through the horrors of the war with spontaneous jubilation. Between 1648 and 1650, in 174 places – mainly in southern Germany and mainly on the occasion of the final departure of the garrisons – peace was celebrated with joyful festivities. And soon the first signs of economic recovery could be registered. Those who had survived profited from the general decline of population numbers because their chances to make a living and marry earlier in life than had been the rule had improved.

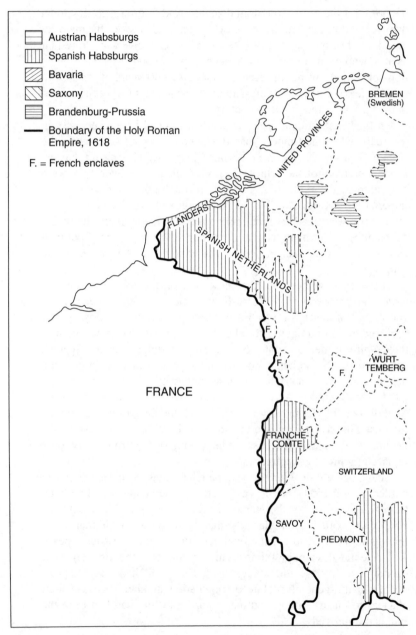

Map 3 Germany after 1648 (adapted from Ronald G. Asch, *The Thirty Years War:*

The Holy Roman Empire and Europe, 1618–1648 (Basingstoke, 1997), pp. xii–xiii).

51

THE LONG-TERM EFFECTS OF 1648

On the whole it was a long way back to normality. The framework and the structure of economic relations had been destroyed, or at least badly damaged, on the regional as well as on the international level. And at the same time economic recovery implied a hidden but long-lasting setback – at least in the agrarian sector: for 'back to normal' meant back to traditional means of cultivation and production, to the techniques and patterns of the rural society of the past. In other countries the general population growth had effected change and modernization in order to avoid disaster. But in Germany this pressure had been relieved by the war and it could afford to stay 'backward' (compared to the Dutch Republic, to England, to France) for more than a century to come.

But war and peace had determined the further course of German history not only in the field of economics. The war of religion was over, which meant that the gulf between Catholic and Protestant Germany was to stay and was to influence culture and politics up the the present day. This also meant that in comparison to most great European states the Empire was not based on confessional conformity but on the co-existence of different confessions. And though confessional antagonisms would remain a constant factor in German politics, yet the preconditions for the development of certain forms of religious toleration were provided. With this development, hopes for the restitution of a uniform Christian dogma had been dashed for ever. And this was the reason for the outrage of Pope Innocent X, who ordered his envoy to denounce the settlement and declared the Treaties of Munster and Osnabrück as null and void.

As in the field of religion, where the peace had established confessional diversity, so in the field of politics particularism, the principle of leaving each member of the Empire free to govern itself and promote its own interest, was reaffirmed. And at the same time the position and power of the territorial states had been significantly enhanced. In the wake of the war the scope of governmental activity was greatly increased; greater resources were at the disposal of the rulers because throughout the Empire the level of taxation had risen during the war. From this point some German principalities became determined to try to achieve the status of a European power.

Nevertheless, in spite of increased particularism the Holy Roman Empire of the German Nation did not cease to exist. Though unable to compete with the political energy and efficiency of the modern European monarchical states, it upheld the claim to unite all its members in an overarching common system of custom and law. Rulers as well as their subjects stood under the jurisdiction of the Empire's supreme law courts: the Empire's Chamber Court and the Aulic Council (at the Emperor's seat in Vienna). And at least on the level of regional and local affairs, the Empire could still act as judge and umpire to guard political and social stability. This applied especially to the patchwork regions of the Empire – like south-western Germany with its countless small political units of free towns, ecclesiastical and secular principalities and the numerous tiny lordships of imperial knights.

In a European context the peculiar constitution of the Empire was to guarantee that no powerful political force would establish itself in the centre of Europe. It became a precondition for the security of Germany's political neighbours as it ensured that no German emperor would from now on be able to dominate the rest of Europe. Instead Germany would serve as a buffer zone – and perhaps as a battlefield again – between the states on the periphery, such as France and the Dutch Republic in the west, Sweden and Denmark in the north, Russia and Poland in the east and the Ottoman Empire in the south-east. In this respect the Treaty of Westphalia served as a fundamental law of a new system of relationships between the European powers.

But the Thirty Years' War and the Peace of Westphalia exerted their most formidable and long-lasting impact on the collective memory of the peoples of Germany and on the gradual formation of a national consciousness. It constitutes one of the many paradoxes of the course of German history, that though the results of the war added heavily to diversity, division and even disunity, the remembrance of the war acted as a unifying factor. The memories handed down by oral tradition from generation to generation kept alive the Thirty Years' War's horrors as a common experience in all the German countries. Later these were seen as a national catastrophe, as the consequence of inner strife which finally resulted in the triumph of overweening foreign powers who chose Germany as their battlefield. And though in its time (and up to the end of the eighteenth century) many regarded the Treaty of 1648 as the foundation of long-lasting peace and stability, others thought it to be the result of utter defeat and humiliation and the source of future weakness and insignificance. Particularly in the eyes of those German nineteenth-century historians who carried the flag of nationalism, the

Thirty Years' War and the Peace of Westphalia became a national trauma – a long-term mortgage which could only be settled after two centuries of crippling payment.

However, to concentrate on the Thirty Years' War as a national catastrophe is to ignore the fact that to a certain extent it can be seen as part of a 'general crisis of seventeenth-century Europe'. Besides armed contests between Europe's kings and republics there was civil war on the Iberian Peninsula, where Catalonia and Portugal rose against the King of Spain, and later on, civil war in England, which led to the first revolution in modern European history. And before open war broke out in Germany and elsewhere there had been many signs of social unrest, due to the gradual breakdown of traditional economic and social structures under the growing pressure of continuous demographic growth between 1500 and 1600.

Yet, it remains a matter of speculation to establish clear correlations between such trends and tensions on the one side and confessional conflict and political crisis in Germany on the other. Instead of regarding the Thirty Years' War as the consequence of a general European crisis, it is more convincing to argue that it was Germany's war that decisively contributed to the general conflagration in seventeenth-century Europe.

4

Eighteenth-Century
Germany

ABSOLUTISM

The period of European history which stretches from the Peace of
Westphalia up to the outbreak of the French Revolution has often been
labelled the Age of Absolutism. But usually the realities of history defy
the degree of uniformity suggested by such a label. Instead, they present
an enormous variety of political systems in Europe, ranging from a
decentralized republican confederation like Switzerland, at one end of the
scale, to extreme autocracies like the Ottoman Empire or Russia, at the
other. And there were also variations within the time-span of a century –
when, for example, England changed its constitution from a republic
under Oliver Cromwell to near absolutism under the late Stuart kings.

Nevertheless, 'absolutism' points to certain peculiar trends and
features which, taken together, mark a new stage in the development
of the forms of political organization of societies, especially in Central
and Western Europe. The model was provided by France. During the
long reign of Louis XIV (1643–1715) a formidable concentration of
the power of the centralized state was achieved at the expense of
entrenched privileges of the provinces and the nobility, and this power
was the personal power of the monarch. He did not only represent the
state but he incorporated the state – 'l'état c'est moi', as Louis was
supposed to have said. This process did not take place only as a correc-
tive to the decentralized institutions left over from the medieval era,
but also in reaction to the often violent rifts between the religious
parties of the sixteenth century. To a certain extent European absolutism was a result of the confessionalization of Europe.

When the power of the monarch was now defined as 'absolute' (*potestas legibus soluta*) this did not imply justification for unbridled despotism. Though it meant the possession of undivided sovereignty, the sole power of legislation and supreme jurisdiction (which was not curtailed by assemblies of the estates, municipal charters, the privileges of nobles and the clergy), the ruler was still bound to observe the maxims of divine and natural law. And whereas in medieval times the main goal of government had been the preservation of peace, of law and order, now care for the general public welfare was also put on the agenda of the ruler.

A firm basis for the enhanced power of the monarch was provided by a standing army under the sole command of the king. And in order to cope with the manifold tasks and duties of the state, the scope and the efficiency of public central administration had to be extended. At the same time state intervention in the field of economics aimed at growing productivity for the sake of raising more and higher taxes, as it was the main tenet of 'mercantilism' that any increase of political power could only flow from an expanding economy.

Therefore, seventeenth- and eighteenth-century philosophers and politicians regarded the state as a huge mechanism, a machine driven by many interacting cogwheels. And its power was to be reflected by the splendour displayed at the monarch's court. This court served as the focus and mirror of absolutism, as the centre of royal government and the stage for the royal spectacle in which a special role was assigned to the nobility and by which the general public, watching from the distance, was kept in due awe.

With an eye to the 'Age of Reason' in the second half of the eighteenth century, the reigns of monarchs like Frederick the Great of Prussia (1740–86), Joseph II of Austria (1765–90) and even Catherine II of Russia (1762–96) have sometimes been labelled as examples of 'enlightened absolutism'. Here the ruler proclaimed the reasonable tenets of the Enlightenment as the targets of his government. To serve this purpose, Frederick the Great even invited the most prominent philosopher of his time, Voltaire, to his court. And he did not regard himself any longer as the incorporation of the state ('L'état c'est moi') but rather as the foremost servant of the state ('Le roi le premier serviteur de l'état'). Yet, this did not contradict rulers' roles as autocrats, who were in no way limited in the execution of their powers by any checks or balances. On the contrary, the more they intended or at least proclaimed to act in the interest of public welfare, the more they saw it as their duty to control and regulate society, to interfere with the private lives of their subjects.

Of course, neither classical absolutism nor enlightened absolutism were ever fully put into practice, nor did they ever achieve complete success. Even in France there continued to exist new and old institutions side by side. And in many countries communities, social groups or even whole regions succeeded in preserving old medieval privileges. But, on the other hand, the ideal of absolute monarchy provided important guidelines and served for more than a century as the main point of reference for good government. It was the blueprint for the machinery of the modern state: a rationally constructed array of institutions, set into motion and controlled by a monarch as the sole executor of the coercive power necessary for external security and internal welfare.

THE 'MONSTROSITY' OF THE EMPIRE

In this context of absolutism the Holy Roman Empire of the German Nation – which, according to the French philosopher Voltaire was neither holy, nor Roman, nor an empire – proved to be the exception to the standard rule. The nature and features of its constitution, as it had finally been shaped by the Peace Treaty of Westphalia, defied any exact definition by contemporary commentators who were used to apply the traditional categories of public law. As it was neither a federation of sovereign states nor a limited monarchy the great lawyer Samuel Pufendorf labelled it 'an irregular monster'.

In the Age of Absolutism the Emperor did not wield sovereign power within the Empire. On the contrary: the princely estates of the Empire, i.e. the rulers in the territories, jealously watched over the inviolability of their newly gained sovereignty. They even formed alliances with one another and with foreign powers like France in order to avert or at least to restrain another rise of imperial power: for example in 1658, when under the leadership of the Elector of Mainz, the main principalities of southern and western Germany joined in the 'League of the Rhine' (*Rheinbund*) to balance the rising influence of the newly elected Emperor Leopold I.

Thus, in obvious contrast to the 'modern' national monarchies of Western Europe the Empire lacked a centre of political gravity. There was no capital. Vienna on the fringe of the Empire had gained importance as the seat of the Habsburg rulers, who, though they were also German emperors, to a great extent based their power on their lands outside the borders of the Empire. And when in 1663 the imperial city of Regensburg on the Danube became the seat of the Diet of the Empire, which from now on sat in permanence as a congress of the ambassadors of the Estates of the Empire, it never gained the status and importance of a political point of focus.

Now even more than before the outbreak of the Thirty Years' War the Empire as a working unit – as the protector of the small and the weak, as the guardian of peace, law and order – was reduced to the regions of the south-west with its hundreds of tiny territories and petty rulers. And though a number of German historians have recently stressed the importance of the longevity of its institutions and its function as a model for supranational federal institutions to come, there is no denying the fact that in the context of general political, economic and social European developments the Empire remained an island of stagnation.

THE TERRITORIAL STATES

The Empire with its complicated institutions and cumbersome procedures resembled an erratic block of past traditions which did not fit into the picture of monarchical absolutism. But many German princes tried to organize their territories along the lines of the great example set by the reign of Louis XIV in France. In the field of politics the main feature of this trend was the attempt to concentrate power in the hands of the ruler by reducing the rights and privileges of the assemblies of the representatives of the nobility, the clergy and the townships of the states. Firstly, this meant abolishing the privilege of these estates to grant taxes, which in the course of the seventeenth and eighteenth centuries was achieved in most principalities of the Empire. In their struggle for unmitigated political power the princes even made use of the Empire by making the Imperial Diet pass resolutions or statutes on their behalf which put the estates under the obligation to grant all taxes that in one way or another contributed to the fulfilment of their masters' military commitments towards the Empire. Thus the strong position of the estates of the Empire contributed to the weakening of the position of the territorial estates.

Apart from this policy of reducing the power and the privileges of the assemblies, the administrations of most German states were centralized and modernized; even small territories kept standing armies, if not for any other purpose than to be regularly put on parade; and some petty despots in their miniature principalities tried to ape the luxurious splendour of Versailles, with the result that today many a former 'capital' can boast its own opera house, theatre, picture gallery and museum. It was during the Age of Absolutism that the foundations were laid for a remarkable cultural diversity as a significant feature of Germany.

Naturally, in Germany as in the whole of Europe, there was a wide variation in how the idea of absolutism shaped the practical realities of government. In some countries, like Mecklenburg, Hanover, Hesse-Kassel or Württemberg, the estates were able to preserve their power and privileges; in others, like the Palatine, they were totally abolished. But in most principalities their political role – mainly their right to grant taxes and manage the public debt – was palpably reduced. Though this meant the extension of princely power at the expense of the political position of the nobility, it did not affect the traditional place of this nobility at the top of the social hierarchy. In most German states a new and firm alliance between the prince and the nobility was formed. The nobles succeeded in adapting to a new political framework by offering their services in leading positions of the army and the administration and they gathered at the seat of the ruler to compete for his favours and to adorn his court. So the gulf which separated them from the ordinary citizen and the peasant was as deep as ever.

The rise of the German territorial states resulted in the larger of them trying to fill the gap that had been left by the decline of the Empire as a key figure in the game of European politics. In this field there was no Germany but there were Habsburg and Bavaria and Saxony and Hanover and Prussia. Nearly all of them were situated in the border zones of the Empire and most of them, in order to add to their political weight, tended to expand beyond the imperial frontiers. Stagnation ruled in the centre of the Empire – the dynamic forces of German politics were active on the periphery.

AUSTRIA

After the Peace of Westphalia the only state of European standing was Austria, ruled by the imperial Habsburg dynasty. Although in the course of the Thirty Years' War the Emperor had not succeeded in achieving undisputed domination of the Empire, he had at least strengthened his position in the various lands attached to his dynasty, in line with the general tenets of monarchical absolutism.

In comparison to the sixteenth century, when Charles V had divided his kingdoms between a Spanish and an Austrian line, the centre of gravity of Habsburg's power had now shifted to the south-east. When in the second half of the seventeenth century France started to expand on its eastern frontier, Habsburg's losses in the west, as in Alsace-Lorraine, were soon balanced by gains in the east. And in 1665 the fortunes of hereditary succession at last resulted in a situation in which all the possessions of the German branches of the Habsburg dynasty were united in the hands of just one ruler: Leopold I (1657–1705) who was also King of Bohemia and Moravia. Moreover, in 1688 the Hungarian estates acknowledged the hereditary right of the Habsburg dynasty to the Crown of Hungary.

This was the result of victorious campaigns against the Ottoman Empire between 1683 – when the Turks for the last time laid siege to Vienna – and 1718, when after the Peace of Passarowitz the gains of the Habsburg Empire even included Serbia. These wars laid the foundations for renewed greatness. A skilful political propaganda campaign launched by the imperial court assigned to the Emperor the role of the defender of Christian Europe against the 'hordes of heathen muslims'. And whereas the defeats by Louis XIV between 1668 and 1697 were ascribed to the weakness of the Empire, the victories against the Ottoman Sultan were celebrated as successes of the Habsburg ruler, who began to draw a distinctive line between the rising state of Austria and the ailing Empire – above all, when after the gains in the south-east a massive block of lands lay beyond the borders of the German Empire.

Thus, after the decline of imperial power at the end of the Thirty Years' War, Habsburg regained the status of full membership in the concert of the Great Powers of Europe towards the end of the seventeenth century. This was achieved despite the setbacks which resulted from having to fight war on two fronts: France in the west and the Ottoman Empire in the south-east. But when one of the great military leaders of the age – Eugene, Prince of Savoy – entered the service of Emperor Leopold I, and when England under William III became Habsburg's main ally in the long struggle against Louis XIV, France's ambitions were trimmed for the first time and after 1697 she even had to abandon some of her recent gains, like the Duchy of Lorraine. Finally, at the end of the War of the Spanish Succession (1701–13), Austria had also regained a strong foothold in Southern and Western Europe, because now it again held the Spanish Netherlands as well as Naples, Milan and Sardinia in Italy. When at the turn of the century Emperor Charles VI was among the great powers of Europe, it was not because he was head of the Empire but because he was head of the House of Habsburg.

Yet Austria's strength rested on precarious foundations. The realm of the Habsburg rulers was not a centralized state nor a working unit on the basis of a political federation, but until the beginning of the nineteenth century it remained a conglomeration of different kingdoms and crown lands, held together only by a common ruling dynasty. And because this dynastic link served as the main unifying element, Emperor Charles VI went to great lengths to preserve the unity of his realm. As there was no male heir in the direct line he tried to secure the succession of his daughter Maria Theresia with the so-called 'Pragmatic Sanction' of 1713, a statute which at the same time implied the indivisibility of his empire and which was finally acknowledged as a fundamental law by the estates of all of his kingdoms.

The second important common bond connecting the different parts of the Habsburg Empire was religion. Apart from some exemptions for the Silesian province, Protestantism was rigorously eradicated. Austria became one of the foremost Catholic states in Europe, where the imperial court and government always acted in close alliance with the Church of the Counter-Reformation.

On the other hand, in spite of many efforts, Austria – as this empire began to be called towards the end of the seventeenth century – only partially succeeded in putting the tenets of absolutism into practice. Though in several parts of the Habsburg Empire the power of the assemblies of the nobility had been curtailed, in most of them they had retained their traditional say in the sphere of taxation. And Hungary would remain a totally different country altogether until the dissolution of the Habsburg Empire after the First World War. Above all Austria lacked any form of administrative unity and most of the time it suffered from inadequate financial resources. A huge public debt was amassed – a fundamental weakness which again and again seriously damaged the military strength of the Habsburg Empire at the most critical moments of its history.

BAVARIA, SAXONY AND HANOVER

Though the Emperor's position had been further reduced by the Treaty of Westphalia, he still played the leading role in German politics – particularly in the southern region of Germany – not only as head of the Empire, but also as head of the Catholic party. This was the source of the long-lasting conflict between Austria and Bavaria, which was more or less enclosed by Habsburg territories and which, too, aspired to the status of a European power in its own right.

Early on, the House of Wittelsbach had decided to stem the tide of the Reformation and as head of the Catholic *Liga* Bavaria joined forces with the Emperor at the beginning of the Thirty Years' War. As his closest and most influential ally its fortunes thrived: in 1623 Bavaria's ruler Maximilian I was finally raised to the status of an elector and five years later Bavaria expanded towards the north by adding the Upper Palatinate to its territory. Moreover, since 1583 and for nearly 200 years the Wittelsbach family had been in continuous possession of the See of Cologne, so that in fact it controlled two electorates. Government was reformed according to the maxims of absolutism. The influence of the estates was minimized and Maximilian I introduced a modern centralized administration.

In 1697 Bavaria found itself on the brink of entering the circle of the great European powers when, trying to arrive at a satisfactory solution to the difficult problem of the Spanish succession, France, England and the Netherlands supported the claim of a Wittelsbach Prince for the vacant throne in Madrid. And although the candidate died prematurely in 1699, this aggravated tensions of long standing with Habsburg, which had always stood in the way of any further expansion of Bavarian influence in southern Germany.

In the context of the long-lasting rivalry between France and Habsburg, the Bavarian–Habsburg antagonism made the Wittelsbach rulers France's natural allies – first as member of the Rhenish Alliance and later in the War of the Spanish Succession. And it was with French assistance that later a Bavarian Elector was even elected Emperor Charles VII (1742–5; the only short interruption in the long line of Habsburg emperors). But in spite of all its efforts to rise to the level of the leading European states, Bavaria remained a second-rate power. On the whole, Bavarian history of the seventeenth and eighteenth centuries is a history of frustrated ambitions.

In contrast to the political constellation in the southern half of the

Empire, where the Emperor still wielded considerable power, his influence in the Protestant north was minimal. Instead, this vacuum was filled by the rivalry of three rising territorial states: Prussia, Hanover and Saxony. All three of them were competing not only for a dominant position in Northern Germany, but also trying to achieve the rank and status of a European power.

At first Saxony led the race. Since the Middle Ages the name of the ancient dukedom of the Saxon kings and the title of the Elector had finally been transferred to the House of Wettin, with domains on both sides of the river Elbe south of Magdeburg. During the second half of the sixteenth century the Elector of Saxony assumed the role of the leader of the Protestant camp within the Empire. Later, during the Thirty Years' War, further lands in the east were acquired and with the reign of Frederick August I (August 'the Strong') absolutism was put into practice.

A considerable upgrading in status was achieved when the Elector of Saxony, with the support of Austria, was elected King of Poland in 1697. The union of the two crowns lasted until 1763 and the splendour displayed at the court of Dresden soon outshone that of his Prussian rival in Berlin. But wearing the crown of Poland implied being involved in the great Nordic War (1700–21), with disastrous consequences not only for Poland but also for Saxony. Even a strong economy, flourishing on the basis of rich natural resources, could only slowly repair the damage inflicted on the country by the political adventures of its ruler. And when after 1740 Saxony fell victim to the aggressive policy of Prussia it was finally reduced to the status of a second-rate German power.

As the name of Saxony was related to the powerful medieval principality in northern Germany, so the dynasty of the House of Hanover stood in direct line to the powerful Guelph family, who had been rulers of the medieval Dukedom of Saxony since 1137. But after Henry the Lion had been deposed and exiled by Emperor Frederick I in 1180, the Guelphs had been reduced to the rule of Brunswick-Lüneburg. Only towards the end of the seventeenth century did the younger branch of this house begin to play an important role in northern German politics again, when Ernest August of Hanover not only organized effective government in his lands but also gained electoral status within the Empire in 1692, and in 1705 reunited Hanover with the even larger state of Celle. His marriage to Sophia, the granddaughter of James I of England, turned out to be of even greater importance, because according to the provisions of the Act of Settlement his son George succeeded Queen Anne at her death in 1714 as George I of Great Britain. This personal union was to last until 1837 when the Salic Law of succession prevented Queen Victoria from retaining Hanover and it passed to her uncle, Ernest Augustus, Duke of Cumberland.

Hanover soon obtained benefit from the British connection when in 1720 it could add Bremen and Verden – formerly under Danish rule – to its territory. Many Britons, however, regarded this 'despicable electorate' – as William Pitt called it – as a heavy burden: it severely hampered their choices and decisions in the field of foreign policy because it was almost defenceless against French or Prussian attack. And although the long connection between the two countries left few traces, it contributed to a further internationalization of German politics, which by this union, even more than in the case of Saxony–Poland, was from now on more closely linked to the Concert of the Great European Powers.

THE RISE OF PRUSSIA

In the end it was Prussia which won the race for hegemony in northern Germany. In the beginning there was the Electorate of Brandenburg, which in 1415 came into the possession of the counts of Hohenzollern from southern Germany near Nuremberg – the ancestors of a dynasty which was to reign until the last German *Kaiser*, William II, was forced to abdicate in 1918. In tenacious pursuit of dynastic policies, especially by means of testamentary contracts, they considerably expanded the territory of the old March of Brandenburg. The most important gains before the outbreak of the Thirty Years' War were the lands of Cleve, Mark and Ravensberg between the lower Rhine and Weser in the west (1614) and Ducal Prussia (the territory of the former Teutonic Order) in the east (1618). By these acquisitions the Hohenzollern rulers had doubled the size of their domains and from now on they enjoyed the twin titles of Elector of Brandenburg and Duke of Prussia.

With the Treaty of Westphalia Frederick William, the 'Great Elector' (1640–88), added the eastern part of Pomerania as well as further lands in the west (Minden and later Magdeburg) to the possessions of his crown. And by the Treaty of Stockholm at the end of the

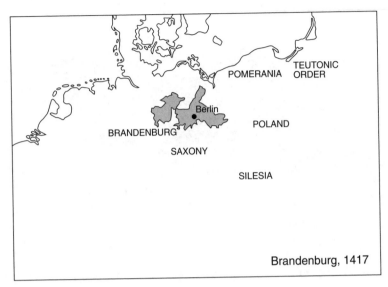

(a)

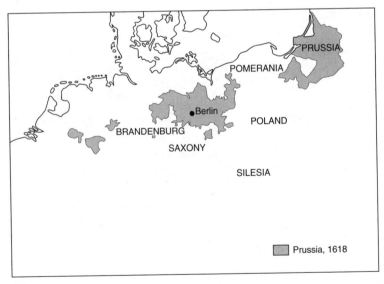

(b)

Map 4(a) to (h) The rise of Prussia (adapted form *Preußen – Versuch einer Bilanz. Eine Ausstellung der Berliner Festspiele GmbH*, 5 vols (Reinbek, 1981), pp. 31–9).

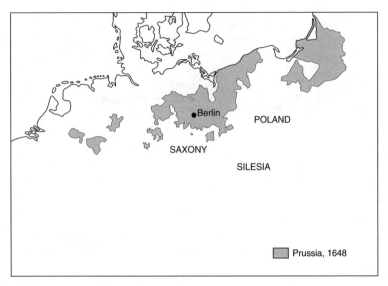

(c)

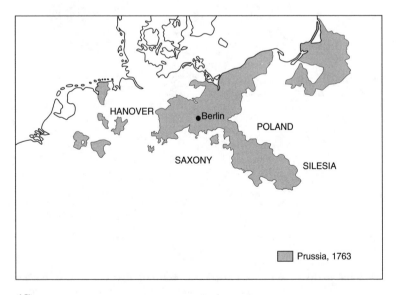

(d)

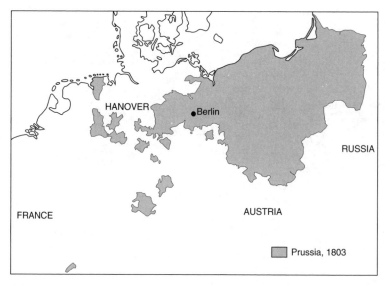

(e)

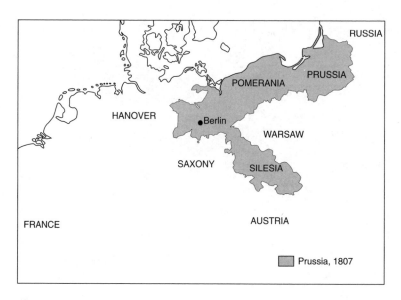

(f)

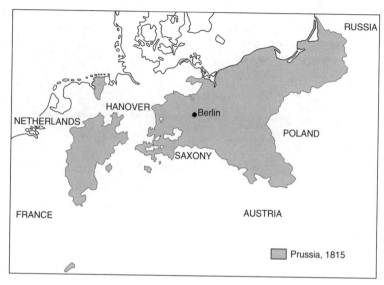

(g)

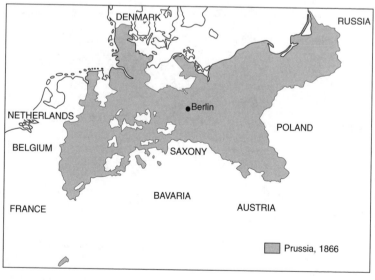

(h)

great Nordic War in 1720 Prussia finally also got the western part of Pomerania.

Elevation in status was also achieved. After his rival in Saxony, Augustus 'the Strong', had been elected King of Poland, the Elector of Brandenburg, Frederick III, with the consent of Emperor Charles VI, crowned himself 'King in Prussia' (1701), a title which – as Prussia was situated beyond the borders of the Empire – claimed equality in rank with the other European monarchs and soon served as the main symbol for the political union of so many different lands.

The dispersion and the disparity of these parts provided extremely difficult preconditions for Prussian politics. This specific geographical location – so many frontiers shared with so many neighbouring states – required great caution in the field of foreign policy and often led to sudden shifts and changes of alliances. And to form a territorial block of the major parts remained the supreme goal of Prussian politics, though it was only achieved in 1866.

Meanwhile it was of prime importance to subject the different parts to the uniform standards of monarchical government. In Prussia, more than elsewhere, it was essential for the survival of the state to put the main tenets of absolutism into practice, which meant: to reduce the power of the estates in the different territories, to establish an efficient central administration and to build up a powerful standing army. All this was achieved in the reigns of the Great Elector and King Frederick William I (1713–40).

The result was the Prussian type of military absolutism based on an efficient bureaucratic administration. In this militarized polity the army formed the nucleus of the state. It had been Frederick William I in particular who had decided on the development of a formidable military apparatus and had increased the size of the fighting forces from about 30,000 at the time of the Great Elector's death to 83,000 in 1740. Now Prussia, though tenth among the European states with regard to its territory and only on rank thirteen as far as its population was concerned, came fourth in military strength. At the same time, the principle of military discipline, the chain of command and obedience, was made the backbone of a centralized administration which was organized along the lines of efficiency and parsimony.

Because Prussia was not a rich country, all her resources had to be stretched to the limit in order to finance its huge army. And as the military budget accounted for the bulk of public expenditure, austerity reigned at the court of Frederick William I. Berlin displayed none of the lavish splendours of luxurious culture usually to be associated with princely absolutism. Instead, as the result of general scarcity, seriousness and severity set the tone not only at court, but in public life in general and soon were to be classified as typical traits of the Prussian character.

In Prussia as elsewhere the successful introduction and establishment of absolutism implied a palpable reduction of the political role and influence of the nobility. The Great Elector had won decisive victories when he deprived the estates of their right to vote taxes for military purposes and of their say in the appointment to key posts in the public administration. But this deprivation of political rights and power was partly compensated for by the fact that local government in the rural districts was totally left in the hands of the *Junker* – the Prussian gentry. As owners of often vast estates they wielded more or less absolute power over the serfs on their soil. As lords of the manor they not only usually enjoyed the unlimited labour services of their tenants but also policed them, sat in judgement upon them and even regulated matters concerning their private lives, for example when their assent for marriage was required. And, occasionally, the lord of the manor even was the commanding officer of those of his tenants who were to serve as soldiers at times of war.

Thus, the nobility became an essential element in the political and social structure of the Prussian state, because the Crown could finally persuade them to regard service to their king not only as a duty but as a moral obligation and as a point of honour as well. The *Junker* as a warrior caste became the main supporting pillar of the Prussian monarchy. In exchange, their social privileges were guaranteed by the king: not only the posts of officers in the army, but also high-ranking positions at court and in the administration were mainly filled by members of the nobility. Until the end of the monarchy the aristocratic soldier would remain the role model of Prussian society.

Throughout the first decades of the eighteenth century the political situation in Germany was determined by Austrian pre-eminence in the south and an uneasy equilibrium between Saxony, Hanover and Prussia in the north. However, a decisive change took place in 1740, when Prussia suddenly unleashed the forces Frederick William I had so carefully built up and organized. When he died in 1740, the place of Europe's foremost 'drillmaster' was taken by his son, Frederick II, who was to become the foremost general of his age. Only six months after he had succeeded his father to the throne he opened up war against Austria and in a short and highly successful campaign seized the rich province of Silesia.

This was done in blatant violation of the laws of the empire by a young ambitious king, eager to have 'his rendezvous with fame'. His success was also due to the fact that in the same year Emperor Charles VI had died without leaving a male heir to his throne, so that Frederick's coup marked the beginning of a military conflict in which nearly all the major powers were involved: the War of the Austrian succession. And it took three wars until in 1763, at the end of the Seven Years' War, Austria finally acknowledged the loss of Silesia and Prussia had definitely risen to the ranks of the Great Powers of Europe.

In the meantime, a fundamental change in the pattern of alliances had taken place which turned the political constellation of the continent upside down. From the end of the fifteenth well into the eighteenth century the Habsburg–French antagonism had been a constant factor in determining the formation of different camps in times of war. But now it was replaced by growing British–French antagonism as a result of the increasing rivalry of the two powers in North America as well as in India. This is why, between 1742 and 1763, the European wars seemed to be a mere extension of or even a footnote to the first stage of this seminal struggle fought overseas between two great powers striving for colonial supremacy.

At the same time, and as French aspirations to hegemony in Europe had been curtailed with the outcome of the War of Spanish Succession, the reconquest of Silesia and the reduction of Prussia gained top priority for Austrian foreign policy. Thus, at the outbreak of the Seven Years' War on the continent, which again was started by Prussia with a sudden assault on Saxony, Frederick II had to take on the formidable coalition of France and Russia as Austria's main allies, while he himself was only supported by Britain, which needed protection of their king's electorate against French invasion. Yet, in a long and bloody war, with Prussian losses of half a million people – the highest since the Thirty Years' War – Frederick held his ground against all odds to be henceforth awarded the epithet of 'Great'.

This spectacular success was, indeed, to a great extent his personal achievement, first of all because he led the war as *le prince connétable*, as the warrior king who was his own commanding general and who soon turned out to be an outstanding strategist and tactician. But in spite of numerous brilliant victories and in spite of the endurance and tenacity by which he survived some crushing defeats, in the end he seemed to be on the brink of losing the war when in 1762 British subsidies stopped and the Russians were poised to take Berlin. He was saved by the death of the Russian Empress Elizabeth and the immediate truce now offered by her successor who was an ardent admirer of the Prussian king.

Peace soon followed (1763) as the result of general exhaustion of the warring sides and finally confirmed the Prussian acquisition of Silesia. But Frederick had gained more than just an extremely valuable province; he had raised Prussia to the status of one of the members of the Concert of the Great European Powers. And he had achieved this in the teeth of his enemies, who at the beginning of the war were determined not only to regain territory previously lost, but had aimed at the annihilation of Prussia as a political upstart and troublemaker who had severely unbalanced the balance of power in Europe.

After success in war Frederick turned to peaceful diplomacy to make further territorial gains. Acting in close alliance now with Russia he and his successor, as participants in the partitions of Poland in 1772, 1793 and 1795, gained new provinces in the east so that from now on Prussia possessed a common border with Russia, thereby, at last, establishing a consolidated territorial base. However, the greater part of the Prussian kingdom now lay east of the river Oder and 40 per cent of the population were of Slav origin.

A CULTURAL COMMUNITY

In the field of politics there was no Germany, neither in the course of the seventeenth nor of the eighteenth century. The Holy Roman Empire of the German Nation had first shrunk and then ossified into stagnation. Instead, there were numerous states with Austria, Prussia, Saxony, Hanover and Bavaria among them: never united, seldom collaborating but most of the time competing for recognition as powers of European standing. Thus, the long and bitter fight between Frederick and Maria Theresia had not been about a leading role within Germany, but had been a rivalry between two European states.

Yet, despite all these political antagonisms and disparities, the eighteenth century witnessed the beginnings of a national discourse in Germany, similar to that on the eve of the Reformation. There remained a common consciousness of unity, a sense of belonging together, which grew even stronger in the course of the eighteenth

72

century, overarching existing particularistic state forms. It rested upon a common language, upon common historical experiences and traditions and upon common cultural values.

These stirrings of a German national consciousness that was independent of the existence of a national state were mainly manifested in the realm of literature and learning. It was initially the child of an intellectual élite which formed the nucleus and the agency of a cultural nation. According to an estimate of the Berlin bookseller Nicolai, in 1770 there were around 20,000 Germans participating in a national debate on national values like the German language, which was to be defended against an overwhelming influence of French, and on national projects like the foundation of a German national theatre as proposed by the critic and dramatist G. E. Lessing. To them, Goethe as a civil servant was a Saxon minister in Weimar, but as a poet he was a German hero like his compatriot Friedrich Schiller. And as cultural activities at most German courts were still modelled on France and French culture – Fredrick the Great even declined to speak German – this new German national cultural community was the child of the new rising middle classes. Reflections on the peculiarities and especially on the values of a German culture automatically led to criticism of and even opposition to those who dominated fashion at those princely courts.

This points to the fact that a cultural nation cannot remain completely separate from the world of politics – sooner or later political implications will have to follow from the observation of national traditions or peculiarities. And in the end a cultural nation represents the first step towards transition to a political nation, and may turn out to be the engine of political unity. This was the case in Germany at least, but in the second half of the eighteenth century there was still a long way to go.

But those who started looking on Germany as a political force looked at the empire and met with disappointment and frustration. The well-known pamphleteer Friedrich Carl von Moser, in his little book 'On the German National Spirit' (1766), complained that the Germans, though 'a people united by a common name and a common language' and virtually destined to provide leadership to the whole of Europe, had in the course of the last centuries 'fallen prey to their neighbours and held by them in contemptuous ridicule' because they are torn apart by inner strife – 'a people: great and at the same time despised, potentially happy but in fact deplorable'.[1] As soon as the nascent national consciousness of the Germans turned to the sphere of politics it ran the danger of giving way to a general inferiority complex; here the trauma of 1648, the feeling of being victimized or at least derided by their neighbours still prevailed with those who were concerned with 'public matters'. However, they began to take pride in their achievements in the realm of culture. The poet Schiller defined 'dignity of the Germans . . . as a moral greatness, attached to the culture and the character of the nation and in no way dependent on the fate of politics'.[2]

But, on the whole, such early stirrings of a German national consciousness could not yet shape the course of history as a political force of its own. Only with hindsight does it gain its importance as the roots of nineteenth-century German nationalism. In fact, it needed a powerful midwife indeed to give birth to the German nation: and this came in the shape of the French Revolution.

5

· · · · · · · ·

Revolution and the Formation of the Nation-State

THE IMPACT OF THE FRENCH REVOLUTION

The French Revolution was never solely a French affair. Since the time of Louis XIV France had been the focus of Europeans' political interest and political imagination. For that reason, from the very outset the great upheaval that began in 1789 soon produced palpable and often violent repercussions all over the continent. As it affected the whole of Europe and in many ways marked the beginning of a new era, it also shaped the course of German history. It did this in two ways: it provided the models and the impetus for political and social modernization and it, literally, cleared the ground for a reallocation of the political forces in Germany as a precondition for a new political landscape and the formation of new political structures.

Initially the events in Paris, the toppling of an absolutist monarchy, the declaration of the rights of man and the draft of a new constitution were greeted with enthusiam by the great majority of German intellectuals. But there were no prospects for revolution in Germany. Most German governments, as well as many admirers of the French Revolution, argued that enlightened rule in their own countries rendered any form of revolution unneccessary. Moreover, admiration soon changed to criticism and even disgust when the revolution accelerated and culminated in the reign of Jacobin terror.

Yet when revolution did change the course of German history, this was initially caused not by the programme and the creed of revolution, but by the French armies invading Germany. For even before events in Paris had reached their climax with the execution of Louis XVI on 21 January 1793, revolutionary France had declared war against Austria. The French saw themselves provoked by a common Austro-Prussian pledge to defend monarchical principles against revolutionary upheavals, and they regarded it as their missionary task to spread the principles of the revolution: to bring liberty and equality to all the peoples of Europe. At the same time they claimed the Rhine as France's 'natural border' in the east. This was the beginning of more than two decades of war in Europe, only occasionally interspersed with short spans of peace, until Napoleon, the heir of the Revolution, was finally defeated in 1815.

During those wars Germany again was one of the main battlefields and, again, for most of the time it suffered defeat and humiliation until it emerged from the turmoil in a new and different shape. Apart from occasional spurious successes of their enemies, the French armies swept all before them. By 1796 they had overrun most of southern Germany. And in March 1798 a delegation of the Empire approved the loss of the left bank of the Rhine at the Congress of Rastatt.

This marked the beginning of the final dissolution of the Holy Roman Empire. For in order to compensate those princes who had lost lands west of the Rhine, it was agreed with the approval of Prussia and Austria to discuss 'secularization' – i.e. the annexation and expropriation – of the ecclesiastical states. In a way those strange religious polities, which had often been under attack from enlightened Germans, had formed one of the main pillars of the gothic structure of the Empire. Now, with unprecedented alacrity a law was passed by the Diet and proclaimed by the Emperor on 27 April 1803, which agreed one of the greatest territorial rearrangements in German history. On the right bank of the Rhine three electorates, 19 bishoprics and 44 abbeys, totalling some 10,000 square kilometres with about three million subjects, disappeared from the political map of Germany. The number of imperial cities was reduced to six.

The beneficiaries of this sweeping reallocation were the larger territorial states: Austria – the former protector of the inner circle of the Empire in general and of the ecclesiastical principalities in particular – Prussia, Bavaria, Baden and Württemberg. All of them were compensated to a far greater extent than their losses on the left bank of the Rhine would have warranted. Prussia, for example, in return for 48 square miles with 127,000 inhabitants acquired 234 square miles with over half a million people. And the middle-sized states like Bavaria, Baden and Württemberg, which would play an important role in the course of nineteenth-century German history, were now given their basic shape.

All these arrangements were made at the expense of the Empire, whose institutions now began to unravel. And when in 1804 Emperor Francis II declared himself to be Hereditary Emperor of Austria, hoping to establish a claim to imperial dignity independent of the Holy Roman Empire of the German Nation, this venerable institution was irrevocably doomed. After another series of crushing military defeats – among them the battle of Austerlitz in December 1805 – Francis was forced by Napoleon to surrender his old imperial title and consequently announced the dissolution of the Empire. This also marked the end of the imperial knights, counts, and the rest of the imperial cities, which lost their special rights and privileges as semi-sovereigns to the expanding territorial states.

This far-reaching transformation of the political map of Germany, which marked not only the end of an era but also the beginnings of a new epoch, had been brought about by the military success of revolutionary France against the continental powers of the *ancien régime*. In this struggle the French victories were only partly due to Napoleon's military genius; in the first place they were the result of the French Revolution. Here a nation in arms swept before her the armies of pressed soldiers of a bygone age, crushing her enemies not only by the sheer force of her numbers but also by her enthusiasm and determination.

At the same time, the defeats of the allies and the ensuing dissolution of the Empire were enhanced by disunity and political rivalries. In 1795 Prussia had abandoned the anti-French coalition and concluded a separate peace because it wanted to concentrate on new territorial gains in the east by joining in the third and final partition of Poland. A short time later nearly all the middle-sized German states were lured into co-operation with France in exchange for substantial acquisitions of new lands, as the outcome of the secularization was to prove. In the War of the Third Coalition (1805) Bavaria, Württemberg and Baden concluded alliance treaties with France and in the wake of the French victory the rulers of Bavaria and Württemberg declared themselves kings with Napoleon's approval. And in July 1806, even before the final liquidation of the Empire, the Confederation of the Rhine was set up under French tutelage by 16 princes of southern and western

Germany – i.e. almost all of Germany outside Austria and Prussia – which was duty-bound to provide Napoleon with military assistance.

Three months later, Prussia, which had stood on the sidelines since 1795, finally saw herself forced into war against France all on her own and, accordingly, was soundly defeated. In 1807, by the Treaty of Tilsit, she lost all her territory west of the Elbe as well as most of her booty from the partitions of Poland, so that she was on the brink of slipping back into the rank of a third-class power. At the beginning of the nineteenth century there was no Germany, but Napoleon as the heir of the French Revolution was the undisputed master of Central Europe.

REVOLUTION BY REFORM

The impact of the Revolution in France did not only effect a radical transformation of the political geography of Germany, it also prompted far-reaching changes in the political and social structures of most German states. And though these might in some respects be labelled as revolutionary changes, they were the results of policies of reform, initiated and executed by governments from above. According to the Prussian minister Count Hardenberg, such policies of reform should aim at 'a revolution in a positive sense, to be made not through violent impulses from below or outside, but through the wisdom of the government . . . this seems to me to be the appropriate form for the spirit of our age'.[1] And though they might have been inspired by the principles and the results of the Revolution in France, in the first place reforms in the German states were the means of coping with the immediate results of those changes that had been effected by the redrawing of the political map of Central Europe. This was achieved in two ways: either *with* France, as in those lands directly annexed by the French and in the states of the Confederation of the Rhine, or *against* France, as in Prussia or Austria.

It was Napoleon's explicit intention to turn the newly created Kingdom of Westphalia, which he had given to his brother Jérome Bonaparte, into a model state as an attractive example of how to realize the promises of the French Revolution – of liberty and equality for all citizens. The attempt to replace traditional feudal structures with a more egalitarian bourgeois society was also meant to guarantee the stability of Napoleon's empire by adapting its new satellite states to the French model.

Similar efforts were made by the governments of the states of the Confederation of the Rhine. Here it was mainly those which had made substantial new gains, i.e. Bavaria, Baden and Württemberg, that tackled the problem of internal consolidation. Their governments began to turn these territories into centralized bureaucratic states by a number of reforms addressing administrative, fiscal and military questions. The main aim of the reformers was to create a dynamic and prosperous society within a rational, homogenous, absolute monarchy.

Naturally, such policies met with stubborn resistance from the nobility with the result that, in the end, considerable deficits in modernization remained, especially in the field of social reform in general and agrarian reform in particular. But on the whole, these French-inspired reforms contributed substantially to the consolidation of those middling states. And apart from the immediate effects of administrative and legal reforms, the fundamental message of the French Revolution – the call for 'liberty, equality and fraternity' – was kept alive in these southern and western regions of Germany and would become one of the main sources of early nineteenth-century German liberalism two decades later.

Whereas Napoleon's German allies attacked the problem of reform in order to deal with the consequences of territorial expansions and to meet the costs of being forced into military alliances with Napoleon, Prussia, and to a certain extent also Austria, introduced reforms in order to overcome the consequences of losses and defeat. Prussia in particular, tottering on the brink of decomposition and even annihilation as the result of military catastrophe, territorial dismemberment, economic disruption and financial ruin after the Peace of Tilsit, realized that comprehensive reforms were necessary if the state was to survive. In order to not only ensure survival but to regain for Prussia a substantial role within Europe, a small group of reformers centred round Baron von Stein and von Hardenberg decided to follow the French model by awakening the 'dormant strengths' of the Prussian people. Dragging along with them an often reluctant King Frederick William III, first Stein as chief minister (1807–8) and then Hardenberg (1810–22) initiated reforms with the aim not of imitating France but rather of preparing Prussia for a final reckoning with Napoleon.

Here, too, reform of administrative structures and the transformation of absolute monarchy into a bureaucratic monarchy was regarded the precondition for turning the state into an effective instrument for social change – the reformers were convinced that only a productive society, freed from the fetters of tradition, could provide the resources necessary for internal renewal and external liberation. To achieve this goal, the famous Edict of October 1807 was to create a free market in land by lifting all feudal restrictions to landownership and abolishing hereditary servitude of the peasant serfs. A financial and tax reform addressed the fiscal crisis caused by huge French demands for indemnity payments and was also intended to foster long-term economic growth according to the classic principles of economic liberalism. In the domain of military reform the reformers were inspired by the French model of *levée en masse*, i.e. the principle that all inhabitants of the state 'are its born defenders', as general Scharnhorst put it: a moderate system of conscription was introduced in 1814. In order to encourage the growth of a general patriotism within a society of self-confident citizens institutions and measures for popular political participation were discussed and Stein's ordinance on urban self-government (1808) included provisions for the election of local officials and representative assemblies. Finally, the question of higher education was addressed by far-reaching reforms of the school and university system.

As Prussian reforms were directed against Napoleon, they were only in part inspired by the French model or the principles of enlightened absolutism; they were also – as Stein's ideas and aims prove – influenced by the patterns of a traditional, hierarchially structured society. Yet these Prussian reforms met with resistance and obstruction not only by the Prussian nobility, who feared for their economic and social privileges, but also by the overwhelming majority of the peasants in the countryside as well as of the artisans in the towns who had little understanding of what was being done in their name. As in the other German states, the policy of reform in Prussia only partially realized its original aims. Thus the gentry either succeeded in retaining crucial instruments of aristocratic power (like patrimonial jurisdiction) or they skilfully adapted to new conditions like those created by the introduction of a modern market economy in rural society.

All things considered, the heritage of the Prussian reforms was an impressive torso. Though some reforms, like those in the military domain, did indeed contribute to Prussia'a survival as a great power, others, like those concerning political participation of the citizenry, remained unfulfilled promises.

Yet, the lasting impact of Prussian reforms on the course of German history can hardly be underestimated. It consisted not so much in the immediate political and social effects of this bundle of laws and ordinances but in the myth they created, which culminated in a historiographical celebration of the reformers' achievements. Prussian reforms were soon regarded as the successful German response and alternative to the French Revolution, as the German way to modernization. In the light of Prussia's final victory over France, the Prussian reforms were seen to provide the basis for Prussia's future claims to political leadership in Germany.

NATIONALISM

The French Revolution did not affect only the political geography of Germany and the political and social structures of the German states – it also had its impact on the political mentality and political culture of the Germans as it proved to be the midwife of modern German nationalism. This new nationalism partly grew out of the emanations of the vague national consciousness of the pre-revolutionary era and can also be linked to proto-nationalist patriotic sentiments, as those inspired by the victories of Frederick the Great. But under the impact of the French Revolution, and especially of French military victories over German armies and French military occupation of German territory, there arose a new concept of a German nation and a new and vigorous sentiment attached to it. Under the impact of the revolution in France and the war against France the discussion and proclamation of national values went beyond the sphere of literary culture and grew into a political movement.

France had demonstrated by the strength of her victorious armies what enormous energies could be activated by a people turned into a nation, i.e. a people united by a common goal. And for the Germans, this common goal was provided by French supremacy, above all by French occupation in many parts of northern Germany: the goal was to liberate German lands by driving Napoleon from German soil. As so often happens in history, nationalist feeling was the result of political humiliation and expressed itself as xenophobic antagonism. Hatred of France provided the unifying bond between all sorts and groups of people and assumed a central role in the emergence of a national consciousness. 'I hate all Frenchmen without exception', proclaimed the pamphleteer Ernst Moritz Arndt, and the poet Heinrich von Kleist called upon his countrymen to dam up the Rhine with the corpses of the slain French. At the same time, others like the philosopher Johann

Gottlieb Fichte preached the singular supremacy of the German nation, whose special mission it was to lead the vanguard of history in its march towards the perfection of mankind.

However, this new political nationalism also implied far-reaching revolutionary tendencies. As the French had demonstrated, a vigorous nation thrived on the political participation of the people and, even more important, it rested on the principle of political equality. And as soon as unity was proclaimed as the supreme political goal, the sovereignty of the separate German states was ignored and even questioned and endangered. When national thinkers tried to fill the void left by the collapse of the Empire and began to develop the vision of a German nation-state, they became dangerous revolutionaries in the eyes of political traditionalists as well as enlightened absolutists.

In the beginning, German nationalism served as a unifying element in the struggle against French supremacy. When the fight for liberation began in 1813, a surge of nationalist rhetoric veiled the differences between various groups with various interests; they were united by their common resistance against French oppression. And though, in fact, the final victory over France was won by the armies of the coalition of the European states of the *ancien régime*, especially by those of the Tsarist Russian Empire, the myth was born that the liberation of Germany was mainly due to universal nationalist enthusiam. The fact that numerous volunteers from all classes of society joined the regular fighting forces – altogether as many as about 30,000 – was seen to be the result of fundamental change, effected mainly by the Prussian reforms. And when in the end Prussian troops, together with Wellington's army, won the decisive victory over Napoleon at Waterloo, Prussia began to be regarded as the true guardian of the nation's heritage.

But even more important for Prussia's future role in Germany was the new geopolitical arrangement of Central Europe after more than two decades of warfare. To this end the rulers or representatives of nearly all European states met in Vienna in 1814.

THE CONGRESS OF VIENNA AND THE REORGANIZATION OF GERMANY

It was not high-flown visions of a new European order but the mechanics of power-politics which determined the outcome of the long discussions of this congress. Though France had been defeated in the end, the impact it had made on the political map of Germany was by no means declared null and void. On the contrary: there was no way back to the motley collection of princes and plenipotentiaries of the old Empire. On the other hand, no way was opened up for the creation of a new German nation-state; instead, the new order was dictated by the interests of the great European states.

In the first place, this meant the reinstatement of the old system of

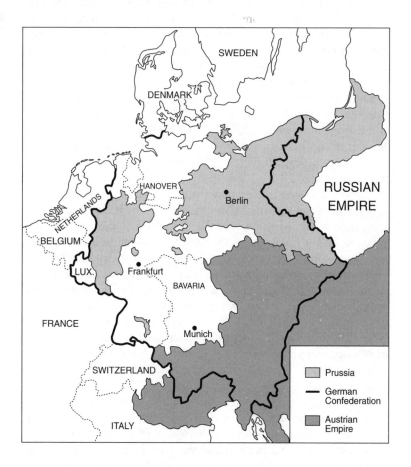

Map 5 The German Confederation, 1815–66 (adapted from Dietrich Orlow, *A History of Modern Germany, 1971 to the Present* (Englewood Cliffs, NJ, 1987, p. 2).

the balance of power, which did not imply the annihilation of France, but only its containment by introducing safeguards against further bouts of aggression.

To this end, Prussia was brought back into Germany to act as the main guardian on the Rhine against the western neighbour. Whereas in the decades before the French Revolution Prussia had continuously expanded towards the east – especially by her gains in the partitions of Poland – now, at the Congress of Vienna, some losses in that region – where a Grand Duchy of Poland as a Russian satellite state had been re-established – were more than compensated by acquisitions in the west: extensive stretches of land in Westphalia and the Rhineland now formed a huge mass of Prussian territory and enabled Berlin to build an arc of influence across northern Central Europe.

The other important geopolitical change in Germany was the reorientation of Habsburg's interests away from the west and towards Southern and South-eastern Europe. With the acquisition of Venice and the regaining of Lombardy it now assumed a new role in Italy. Besides the Balkans the main focus of Austrian policy was henceforth to be found in Northern Italy where even the bulk of its army was to be stationed until 1848.

In the south-west of Germany the middle states – Baden, Bavaria and Württemberg – remained the big winners from Napoleon's reorganization of Germany, because they had deserted their former tutor, protector and ally and changed sides in time, in return for the guarantee of their former territorial gains. Thus, instead of restoring the political map of pre-revolutionary Germany, the impact of the French Revolution was legitimized. Instead of the huge variety of about 1800 independent political units existing within the framework of the old Empire there now remained only 41 sovereign territories. Among these were one empire and five kingdoms, but most of these entities were quite small, in 1818 only seven German states had populations of more than one million and 13 had less than 50,000, among those the free cities of Frankfurt, Bremen and Lübeck.

The next problem that had to be solved was how this Germany, as the central region of Europe, was to be politically organized in order to ensure peace and stability. Another sytem of balancing powers had to be established and institutionalized between the smaller and the larger states and between the two latent rivals in this region: Austria and Prussia. As in 1648, when the Peace of Westphalia was negotiated at Munster and Osnabruck, the Congress of Vienna had to solve the question of how to prevent either the formation of a strong and potentially aggressive political force or the emergence of a political vacuum in the middle of Europe, as either would severely endanger the precarious political equilibrium on the continent.

Mainly on the basis of a draft by the Austrian foreign minister, Count Metternich, the German states agreed in June 1815 on a common constitution for a confederation of the 'sovereign princes and free cities of Germany', as it said in the first article of the document. It was conceived as a 'strong and durable union for the independence of Germany and the peace and equilibrium of Europe' and in article 2, 'the independence and indefeasibility of the separate German states' was declared to be its main aim.

This confederation possessed only one statutory institution, an assembly, the *Bundesversammlung,* which was organized as a diet of delegates appointed and instructed by the governments of the member states. Its seat was Frankfurt and it met either regularly in a small council or in full assembly on special occasions. Austria was given the right to chair the meetings. Procedures were organized in such a way that on fundamental issues the big states could not be outvoted by a united front of the small states, nor could the latter be overwhelmed by their more powerful neighbours. And there were some echoes of the old Empire: only part of the territories of the biggest member states, Prussia and Austria, belonged to the federation whose boundaries were the same as those of the old empire; therefore, more than half of the Habsburg lands and Prussia's most eastern provinces were left outside 'Germany'. On the other hand, there were substantial non-German minorities: the Czechs in Bohemia and Moravia, the Slovenes in the south-east and Italians in South Tyrol. At the same time, three foreign sovereigns were members of this federation of princes: the King of England in his capacity as ruler of Hanover (until 1837), the King of Denmark as Duke of Holstein and the King of the Netherlands for Luxemburg.

On the whole, this new German Confederation was meant to be a factor of stability, a defensive organization: one of the first and most detailed acts of legislation concerned the organization of federal military contingents and the upkeep of common border fortresses on the western frontier. And Metternich, the architect of the constitution, as well as most of the princes who joined it, regarded this German constitution as another bulwark against the dangerous forces of political modernization and social change let loose by the French Revolution.

Though the Act of Confederation contained some vague promises for representative government, freedom of the press and economic unity, these remained a dead letter. There was no catalogue of the rights of man apart from a declaration of equal rights for all Christian confessions and the freedom of movement and settlement for citizens of the German states, but article 14 set down in detail the prescriptions for the protection of the special privileges and property rights of the former imperial aristocracy.

Though the French Revolution had to some extent paved the way to the formation of the future German nation-state – in particular by redrawing the political map of Germany and providing the impulse for reforms in many fields – at the beginning of the nineteenth century this goal was still a long way off and there was no straight road mapped out leading to the German nation-state.

FROM REVOLUTION TO RESTORATION

The specific dynamics of nineteenth-century European history were closely linked to the driving forces of revolution: the Industrial Revolution in the economic sphere and the French Revolution and its offspring in the field of politics. Since the latter did not end in 1814, its energies were not exhausted with Napoleon's final defeat. Revolution was to erupt repeatedly throughout the whole of the century, and in 1830 and 1848 Paris was again the source of convulsions which shook the states of Central Europe and again shaped the course of German history.

In the first stage, between 1789 and 1815, though Germany had been heavily affected by the French Revolution, there was no German revolution following the example set by the events in Paris. Half a century later this was different and the French only supplied the burning match for a keg of powder the Germans had provided themselves. From whatever angle one starts to look at German history in the early nineteenth century, it will always be linked to the concepts of revolution or political modernization.

At first, under the impact of Napoleon's supremacy, reform had been the German reaction to the challenge of revolution. In the states of the Confederation of the Rhine and in Prussia partial modernization had been the result, mainly in the spheres of administrative and economic life. And though all the strength of the nation and the patriotic spirit of the citizens was to be mobilized for the benefit of state and society, no challenge to princely authority was intended. On the contrary: even projects for introducing means and institutions for political participation of certain groups of citizens (like property owners in the Prussian cities) were to enhance the efficiency of the state by harnessing the energies of its people. Since reformers intended to defend the monarchical state against fundamental change, their reforms have been seen as the results of a political strategy of 'defensive modernization'. But as every policy of reform implies change and can entail far-reaching consequences, a new tide set in after 1815: even limited, gradual reform was viewed with suspicion, projects were often annulled or at least shelved, others were stopped or perverted.

In Prussia, Chancellor Hardenberg's plans to deprive the nobility of its political privileges were thwarted by the stubborn resistance of the gentry which, in the end, succeeded in retaining their authority in the rural districts as well as their leading position in the army and the administration. And though in 1815, at the height of the fight for liberation, Prussia's king had promised his people a 'national representation', after the end of the war Metternich succeeded in convincing Frederick William that popular representation was incompatible with the structure of the Prussian monarchy. By 1819, most Prussian reformers had resigned apart from Hardenberg.

Like Prussia, Austria, Hanover and Saxony remained absolute monarchies after 1815 and in Brunswick and Hesse-Cassel the rulers soon bore themselves again in a way reminiscent of the worst days of the *ancien régime*. Austria in particular, where many different ethnic communities were united under the rule of the Habsburg dynasty, had to fear the growth of revolutionary nationalism, which would be boosted by the creation of national representative institutions. This is why, after the victory over revolutionary France, the general answer to revolution was no longer 'reform' but 'restoration', because, as the Duke of Wellington wrote in 1830: 'Beginning reform is beginning revolution.' And though, as in the case of the bygone Empire, the clock could not always be put back, it was at least the aim of men like Count Metternich, who became the embodiment of the politics of his period, to prevent any form of change, so that 'restoration' at least meant 'stagnation'.

Yet, there were some exceptions to this rule. The situation was different in south-western Germany. Here, in the states of the former Confederation of the Rhine, further reforms – even reforms in the sphere of the constitution which could be identified with the tenets of political modernization – were inaugurated and put into practice. By 1820 Baden, Bavaria and Württemberg possessed written constitutions, largely modelled on the 'Charte', the French constitution of 1814. Their most important feature were bicameral representative institutions, with an upper chamber where membership was based on hereditary rights or royal appointment and a second chamber of deputies elected on the basis of a highly restricted franchise by certain categories of voters from the citizenry. These parliaments were endowed with the right to control the budget and to collaborate in matters of legislation. Moreover, the charter for Bavaria, for example, contained a catalogue of basic rights for the people, such as equality before the law and freedom of conscience.

However, this 'constitutionalism', as this form of semi-parliament-arization is usually called, did not imply the breakthrough either of popular sovereignty, or of a parliamentary system as in Britain. Instead, these constitutions had been introduced 'from above' for two reasons:

- to consolidate these states by integrating the diverse new populations acquired in the course of recent territorial expansions;
- to link the massive public debts to the responsibility of the representatives of the propertied section of the population. Otherwise, the power of those parliaments stopped short of control of the government. Ministers continued to be responsible to the prince alone, whose power remained virtually unbroken in most of these states.

In spite of such limitations these constitutions were loopholes in the dam carefully erected to stem the revolutionary tide. Though they had been ordained and enacted by the monarchs, whose *de facto* powers were not substantially curtailed by these constitutions, yet their authority was from now on defined by and bound to the letter of a law which could not be revoked or changed unilaterally by the ruler. His was no longer an absolute power (*potestas legibus soluta*), i.e. a power above and beyond human laws. And – even more important – the newly installed parliamentary institutions could provide a platform from which dangerous ideas could be broadcast throughout the whole of the German Confederation.

However, for more than a decade, up to 1830, the politics of restoration swept all before them. Its success was even heightened by the first stirrings of a revolutionary German nationalism. For some of the enthusiasm of the wars for national liberation still lived on after 1815, particularly among the younger generation who had joined as volunteers in the fight against the French. Many of them were members of gymnastic societies like the one Friedrich Ludwig Jahn had founded in 1811 to mobilize national awareness and resistance to France by paramilitary drill. Other students joined a new style of fraternities, the *Burschenschaften*, which shunned the pleasures of traditional student life and, instead, proclaimed it their task to spearhead a general movement for national unity at a time when political particularism had just been reaffirmed by the Act of Federation.

To this end, students at the university of Jena on 18–19 October 1817 organized a patriotic festival at the Wartburg (where Luther had hidden from his enemies and had translated the Bible) to celebrate the tricentenary of the Reformation and the victory won against Napoleon three years before at Leipzig. Representatives from most German universities took part in this first political demonstration in German history, which culminated in a symbolic act of political defiance when a high-spirited group from Berlin burnt in effigy not only the *Code Napoléon*, but also some books of prominent supporters of the restoration.

This action, and especially the murder of the dramatist August von Kotzebue, an ardent opponent of the fraternities, by Karl Sand, a mentally unbalanced student of theology and member of the *Burschenschaft*, provided Metternich and his allies in Berlin with a most welcome opportunity to crush what they regarded the dangerous stirrings of a revolutionary nationalist movement. The upshot was the issuing of the Decrees of Karlsbad (1819), which ordained close supervision of the universities, investigations of revolutionary activities and, most important of all, a rigid censorship of newspapers and periodicals. When, in a secret session, the Diet of the Federation adopted these stern resolutions as guidelines for its own policy, the German Federation revealed itself as an instrument of restoration politics. In further amendments to the constitution, passed in the following year, the institutional impediments to change were further reinforced, so that the Confederation was finally stripped of all potentially progressive elements that had been part of the original charter.

The policy of the Decrees of Karlsbad succeeded in keeping Germany quiet for a decade. This success was mainly due to the fact that hardly any resistance could be put up as long as Metternich's

Austria and Prussia acted together in close union. But it also revealed the essential weakness of the forces of revolution in Germany at the beginning of the nineteenth century. Only a tiny minority within a restricted public sphere cared for national union and constitutional liberty. It consisted mainly of academics, journalists and poets and was more or less isolated from the mass of the people who were enjoying a most welcome period of peace and tranquillity. Yet, the restoration policy of repression could only delay – not reverse – the rise of revolution as a political force in Germany. This became obvious when in the wake of the second French revolution in July 1830 most German states were affected by outbreaks of popular unrest. In Brunswick a real revolution did occur when the royal palace went up in flames and the despotical Duke Karl II was forced to abdicate. And here as elsewhere in northern Germany new constitutions were granted which guaranteed a certain amount of political participation not only to the nobility but also to parts of the citizenry.

The climax of these renewed stirrings of political opposition was again a public demonstration, similar to the Wartburg Festival of 1817. This time it was a genuine mass meeting – on the morning of 27 May 1832 about 25,000 people gathered on a hilltop in the Palatinate at the foot of the ruins of the castle near the town of Hambach. Well organized by radical journalists, the participants of this political rally were not just academics, but businessmen, farmers, craftsmen and wage-labourers. And some speakers even called for not just a united German nation-state, but a German republic, based on popular sovereignty.

THE 1848 GERMAN REVOLUTION

Thoroughly alarmed by the sheer size of the Hambach Festival and the intense political commitment of those attending, the Diet of the Federation under the guidance of Metternich again introduced repressive measures against political associations, popular meetings and any form of 'revolutionary agitation'. Yet, in the end, this was to no effect and the strategies and efforts of restoration politics could not prevent – when in February 1848 revolution broke out in Paris again – the whole of Germany being shaken by revolutionary upheaval only four weeks later. And because behind the façade of restoration and stagnation multiple change had taken place, there now existed conditions which made it possible in spring 1848 for the revolution to achieve what seemed to be a sweeping victory. Whereas at the dawn of the century only a tiny minority had risen in protest against the re-establishment of monarchical absolutism and political particularism in Germany, now the masses rose in many towns and some rural regions, demonstrating, clamouring and even fighting for change, often led and organized by leaders who were able to outline the aims and targets of revolutionary action. Several significant developments in various fields had combined to advance and accelerate the growth of a revolutionary situation.

First, there was the demographic element, the marked growth of the German population at an ever-increasing rate so that it had almost doubled between 1740 and 1840. In 1816 there were 30 million people living within the frontiers of the Federation and this number rose to 47.5 million in 1867. And this rate of population growth of 56 per cent was even surpassed by Prussia with 88 per cent for the same span of time.

This increase led to growing tensions within the framework of German society. At a time when nearly 90 per cent of the people still lived in the country and about 80 per cent were dependent on agriculture and husbandry (as full-scale industrialization had not yet set in), the existing agrarian economy could not accommodate this huge surge in population, particularly during periods of bad harvests. In Germany as well as in most European countries productive capacities did not grow quickly enough to provide for an expanding population.

In the 1840s it became evident at last that a substantial minority of Germans was permanently destitute. Mass poverty was at the root of the social crisis. To a certain extent this was the legacy of economic modernization which had put the poor at a disadvantage. For example, reforms like Stein's emancipation of the Prussian peasantry had unleashed the forces of the market economy and thus terminated modes of social security provided by the traditional relationship between lord and serf. And in the towns it was mainly the artisans who fell victim to pauperization because here the guild system which had offered them a certain amount of social protection steadily lost ground at a time when more and more labourers from the rural districts migrated into urban areas, and when at the same time demand for their products declined as a consequence of the general economic crisis.

During the late 1840s in particular, growing widespread material deprivation led to consumer protests and labour unrest in many towns and regions, often bordering on political upheaval, as in August 1845 in Leipzig and in April 1847 in Berlin. And though social distress in itself is never a sufficient cause for revolution, it provides the foot soldiers for the fights on the barricades.

The leaders of the revolution came from the growing urban middle class, which became the most dynamic force in early nineteenth-century German society. In certain areas, for example in the Rhineland, this new bourgeoisie was engaged in trade or manufacturing, but the main factor in the rise of this new class was education, which their members set against the privilege of birth of the nobility. They were civil servants, lawyers, clergymen and doctors, most of them educated at one of the numerous universities, and together with the entrepreneurs and merchants and bankers they formed a self-conscious middle class which became the backbone of the German revolution.

And as revolution is not just protest, not just rebellion against oppressive rule, but is always bound to hope and the belief in a better future, to some kind of utopia worth fighting for, those who at first criticized and opposed the politics of restoration and later were among the leaders of the German revolution proclaimed and pursued two main common aims: personal liberty and national unity. In between those two corner-stones of the political programme of the German Revolution a whole range of various and occasionally even contradicting political positions and ideologies were united in their common struggle against the forces of the *ancien régime* and the counter-revolution, ranging from moderate liberalism to radical democracy and even including some forerunners of socialism.

Nearly all of them demanded freedom of the press and freedom of conscience and a unified nation-state; many favoured economic freedom, but others looked to a strong state for protection from either competition or social disorder. And though all called for constitutions as restraints on princely absolutism, differences opened up as soon as the range of political participation of the citizens was to be defined. Most liberals feared democracy, while radicals even advocated republicanism on the basis of the sovereignty of the people; some demanded Western-style parliaments, others associated freedom with a strong administration. Thus, the call for freedom took many forms and appealed to various groups for different reasons, which accounted for the surprising strength of the political opposition in March 1848.

This was also the result of the most important of all changes leading up to the German Revolution: the formation of a public sphere as a frame and a network for political discourse on a national level. It was a remarkable achievement in the teeth of the numerous repressions of restoration politics directed against all kinds of political communication and association. Though political parties were forbidden, after 1830 various crypto-political organizations sprouted all over Germany: there was a widespread revival of Jahn's gymnastic societies with about 90,000 members in the mid-1840s, and the student fraternities had regained their political importance. But there were also Schiller Societies and Luther Clubs, which were obviously politicized; numerous choral societies singing national songs at their gatherings had at least 100,000 members by the end of the 1840s and learned associations held national conferences and proclaimed national aims. Educational and self-help societies raised political awareness among the lower orders and sometimes even became centres of political activity. And journeymen on their travels round Central Europe often carried revolutionary broadsheets in their knapsacks.

At the same time, the debates in the representative assemblies of the constitutional states attracted growing attention when members of the liberal opposition raised questions of fundamental constitutional importance. In particular, the parliament of Baden achieved a kind of national status in this respect and it was here that on 12 February 1848 – i.e. even before the outbreak of the revolution in Paris – a motion was tabled to install a national representative assembly at the Frankfurt Diet.

Finally, revolution was made possible by the crumbling defences of the *ancien régime*. Though the old laws of persecution and repression were still in force and new ones were added by the Assembly of the Federation, because of rivalries among the member states no coordinated confederal action against those who were suspected of being revolutionaries could be organized. In spite of renewed censorship the reading public continued to grow and public debate became more vigorous: the number of books published in Prussia increased by 150 per cent between 1821 and 1840 and by the 1830s Berlin had 60 and Bavaria 100 bookshops. Controls were gradually relaxed under the general impression of imminent crisis, which paralysed the authorities to the same extent as it quickened the forces of opposition. In many ways the ground was prepared for the revolution to come.

When revolution finally came – again in the wake of events in Paris, where in the last week of February 1848 the Orleanist Monarchy fell – it spread with the aid of the telegraph and the railway from

Baden eastward and northward and this time it affected the whole of Germany because, unlike 1830, it did not stop short of Austria and Prussia. On the contrary, it culminated in fights on the barricades in Vienna and Berlin, where a revolution that elsewhere was markedly non-violent claimed its heroes with 300 dead, mostly artisans and workers. At the same time the peasantry rose in those regions where serfdom and feudal privileges were still in force, i.e. mainly in the smaller states of the south.

During those first weeks the revolution gained sweeping victories – the authorities were paralysed and nervous rulers made hasty concessions. In Berlin, though the troops were not actually beaten, they were withdrawn and King Frederick William IV paid homage to the revolutionary martyrs. Everywhere prominent members of the liberal opposition were appointed to form new administrations – the so-called 'March ministries'.

However, the most important aspect of the revolution was that it was a national event: though there were revolutions in Prussia and Austria and Bavaria these were just aspects of a German revolution. Everywhere voices were raised for a pan-German parliament and, indeed, in May elections were held for a German National Assembly in Frankfurt on the basis of a remarkably wide suffrage. And soon this parliament tackled the two fundamental issues of the German Revolution: how to establish national unity and how to secure civil liberty. In less than one year this formidable task had been completed and a constitution had been drawn up for a future German empire, to be organized along the lines of liberalism and federalism.

Yet, this constitution was never to be put into effect. The German revolution ended in failure when the Prussian King Frederick William IV refused to accept the Crown of this new national empire on 24 April 1849. And after the last popular uprisings had been crushed during the weeks of early summer by military force, above all by Prussian troops, a new decade of political reaction set in.

One of the main causes for failure had been the seemingly sweeping success of the revolution in March 1848, which made it 'stop short of the thrones'. Partly out of confusion and partly for tactical reasons rulers acceded to popular wishes, so that their authority seemed heavily damaged. But in fact the revolutionaries were less powerful than they appeared, and the forces of the old order less weak. For the powers retained by the German princes were more or less unbroken, because in most cases they were able to keep their armies intact. Given the military superiority of regular soldiers over untrained and often poorly armed revolutionary fighters on the barricades, this was one of the main reasons for the final success of the counter-revolution.

The initial victory also disguised multiple and occasionally even deep divisions among the revolutionaries. They differed from each other over aims as well as over tactics. As the long and often intense debates of the Frankfurt National Assembly show, most of the time Liberals, ready to compromise and always reluctant revolutionaries, stood against Democrats, who aspired to radical change. Liberals wanted a limited, property-based franchise in a constitutional monarchy as a barrier against social revolution; the Democrats demanded universal male suffrage in a republic.

Besides, issues of power and sovereignty were interlinked with conflicts over the national question and often overlaid by religious, regional and social divisions. Occasionally, such divides led to sporadic outbursts of violence – often the result of thwarted lower-class aspirations – and to further insurrections throughout 1848 and 1849, which fed the growth of anti-revolutionary sentiments within the middle classes, made liberal ministers call for the support of Confederation troops and thus played into the hands of the rising reaction.

Moreover, shrewd concessions by the rulers over certain partial reforms contributed to separating liberals from radical revolutionaries. In Prussia, for example, a constitution was introduced by the king in December 1848 which contributed considerably to satisfying moderate liberal opinion. Similarly, in southern Germany as well as in many parts of the Habsburg Empire peasant discontent was appeased by granting agrarian reforms and abolishing the last feudal residues. Gradually, most of the countryside withdrew from revolution and the peasantry began to turn conservative.

And finally, in comparison with France the German revolution lacked a capital like Paris, a focus of political power which would be the natural target for a revolutionary take-over. Polycentrism was another cause of its weakness.

Thus the revolution in Germany had soon spent its initial energy by fighting on too many fronts. It had to tackle too many issues at the same time, squaring the new German nation with the existing states system of the Federation, defining its borders within the tangle of old established states and new rising nations in Central Europe and working out a constitution in the teeth of opposing political ideologies. In the end, none of its original aims were achieved – neither political liberty nor national unity were established.

Yet, in view of its long-term effects on the course of German history, the revolution was not a complete failure. Though the concept of popular sovereignty had suffered defeat and the road to democracy was blocked for more than half a century, after 1850 almost all German states, even Prussia, had at least some kind of constitution and parliament. And, most important of all: the revolution had again put the problem of the German nation-state on the agenda.

The central importance of the national question was as much cause as effect of the revolution of 1848. National sentiment had grown in Germany, especially after 1840 when France had threatened to regain her 'natural frontier' in the east by annexing the left bank of the Rhine. This had caused an unprecedented surge of national feeling among Germans and the popular song 'They shall not have it, the free German Rhine' became a kind of national anthem. This is why in 1848 the aim of establishing a strong German nation-state united all the parties and became the common denominator of the political revolution. But as soon as the National Assembly sat down to define where the outer borders of Germany were to be drawn and in what manner the members of the Federation were to be integrated into this new state, a string of serious conflicts arose. In Bohemia a Czech national movement emerged and declined to send its representatives to the Frankfurt Parliament, though the province was part of the Federation and had been part of the former Empire. In the north Danes and Germans even went to war over the Duchies of Schleswig and Holstein and in the east in the Prussian province of Posen, German claims had to be reconciled with those of the Poles.

The most pressing question of all, however, soon proved to be whether or how Austria could become part of the new nation-state. Here the majority of the National Assembly had at first favoured the so-called 'greater German' solution, which sought to include the German provinces of the Habsburg Empire. But when this plan ran up against Austrian determination to maintain its empire intact, no other choice was left for the members of the Frankfurt Parliament but to adjust their draft of a pan-German constitution to a 'lesser German' solution, that is, a nation-state as a federal system that preserved the existence of the individual states. Austria was to be left outside and only loosely associated to this new German state. Protestants and liberals, mainly from northern Germany, were advocates of this 'lesser

Germany' and they looked to Prussia as the leading power in a new German empire and its king as a future hereditary emperor.

When Frederick William's rejection of the German crown put an end to the aspirations of all those who had wished to turn revolution into the vehicle for the creation of a new German nation-state, this was only partly due to the king's determination not to accept any constitution emanating from a revolutionary national assembly. At the same time there were sound foreign policy reasons for pulling back: namely Austria's determination not to accept any German state more advanced than the loose Confederation of 1815, as well as the firm resolution of nearly all European powers, especially Britain and Russia, not to have the European system unbalanced by the emergence of a new powerful nation-state in the heart of Europe.

Such was the political legacy of the German revolution for the future of the national movement: to have tested the two alternatives of 'greater' and 'lesser' German concepts and their political implications, and to have discovered that the problem of founding a German nation-state could only be solved in the context of European politics.

THE FOUNDATION OF THE GERMAN NATION-STATE

Though a sovereign German nation had failed to establish the German nation-state all by itself in the course of the German revolution, it took less than another 25 years to place a new German state right into the centre of the political map of Europe. This time, however, it was not the result of political action 'from below' but 'from above' – the outcome of power politics, of diplomacy and warfare. To a certain extent the new Germany can be seen as the by-product of Prussia's victory over Austria, which put an end to more than a century of rivalry between the two major German powers.

As soon as the last insurrectionary movements had been crushed in 1849, both were back at their struggle for mastery in Germany, when Vienna thwarted a last effort of Berlin to organize – in alliance with moderate liberalism – a German Union headed by Prussia during 1849–50. From now on there was continuous rivalry between the two leading powers of the German Confederation, which had been brought to life again after the end of the revolution. Finally, in 1866, the struggle culminated in a kind of German civil war, in which Austria was backed by most members of the Confederation. But in the battle at

Königgrätz (1866) Prussian military superiority carried the day. The struggle which Frederick the Great had begun in 1740 was finally decided. And though Austria was still considered a natural part of Germany by many Germans, from now on (with the dissolution of the old German Federation) it was expelled from Germany, which was to be organized along the lines of what in 1849 had been called the concept for a 'lesser German' solution.

Among Prussia's substantial territorial gains were the electorate of Hesse, the kingdom of Hanover and the Free City of Frankfurt and in the following year, in a first step, the whole of northern Germany was united in a confederation under Prussian leadership. The southern German states were bound to Prussia by military alliances, which they honoured in the Franco-Prussian war of 1870–1. In the wake of another Prussian victory and carried by the tide of national sentiment they, too, became members of the new German Empire – *Das Deutsche Reich* – which was proclaimed at Versailles in January 1871. A new chapter in the history of Germany was opened because now the term 'Germany' did match a single political unit: a German nation-state.

This *Reich* was the result of a complex development, the outcome of a mixture of continuity – like the unfolding industrialization and the ongoing Prussian–Austrian rivalry – and contingency – for example the fact that a skilful as well as ruthless politician like Otto von Bismarck was shaping Prussian politics. Long-term processes – like the growth of German nationalism and the construction of the Prussian customs union – met with the effects of unexpected constellations, like the breakdown of the traditional system of the balance of powers. The latter especially provided the most important prerequisite for the aggrandizement of Prussian power in the shape of the foundation of the *Deutsche Reich*.

In 1871, German unification, which now had been achieved not on the barricades of a national revolution but by the victories of Prussian armies on the battlefields of Bohemia and France, did not provoke the same amount of European resistance as the efforts of the revolution had done in 1848, when Britain and Russia had been on the brink of military intervention over the border conflict between Germany and Denmark. Although he subverted the international order, Bismarck's policy did not cause concerted action by neighbouring powers, because the old equilibrium of the Concert of Europe had disappeared with the Crimean War (1853–6) when France and Britain had blocked

Russian ambitions to expand on the Balkans. A new system, which was to be based on the legitimacy of nation-states and to include Germany and Italy, had yet to emerge. Prussia had benefited from a period of uncertainty and rearrangement in international relations.

Bismarck's success in power politics also contributed decisively to gaining the support of German liberalism, as it was closely intertwined with nationalism. With this Prussia won an important ally because liberal nationalism continued to dominate public opinion in Germany even after the Revolution of 1848. This alliance was a remarkable achievement, because originally Bismarck had been called into office in 1862 to crush liberal resistance to the monarch's violation of the Prussian constitution – he would not accept parliamentary decisions on the question of military reform. As both sides saw principles at stake, matters escalated into a constitutional conflict when Bismarck governed the country against the will of the majority of a parliament which even refused to vote for a regular budget. Political deadlock lasted for four years until two months after the victory over Austria when the majority of Prussian liberals agreed to 'indemnify' the government for its breach of the constitution and formed the 'National Liberal Party'.

Having failed to achieve freedom and national unity at the same time and having learnt that high-flown political ideas like that of a German nation-state could not be realized without the power necessary to enforce them, most liberals were now ready to sacrifice political freedom on the altar of national unity. In particular, those who had fought for a 'lesser Germany' during 1848–9 saw most of their political dreams come true with the inauguration ceremonies of the German Empire at Versailles in 1871. And though at the time being thwarted in their ambitions for parliamentary government, they could still believe that in the long run they would be able to place their own imprint on the new German nation-state.

But liberals were not only impressed by Prussia's power politics and her military prowess – she could also claim considerable success in the field of economic policy. Here even before 1848 Prussia had gained pan-German leadership by slowly and steadily extending her own customs system into a German Customs Union between 1819 and 1834. Originally the product of Prussian geographical division and fiscal interest, by 1842 it embraced more than half the members of the German Federation and as a growing and dynamic free trade area provided an important economic stimulus.

Moreover, as Austria was left outside, this customs union soon could – and for many did – serve as a blueprint for a 'lesser Germany'. And indeed, whereas Austria constantly struggled with financial problems and lagged well behind Prussia in economic development and institutional modernization, the area of the German Customs Union and later the Lesser German Empire became the powerhouse of German economic development. Soon after, the failure of political revolution Germany was transformed by the Industrial Revolution which, to a considerable extent, boosted the formation and the rise of the nineteenth-century German *Reich*.

6

· · · · · ·

Industrialization and Social Change

Fundamental economic change like the Industrial Revolution is always the result of the interplay of many factors and it is seldom possible to distinguish between cause and effect; it is usually a two-way relationship. Thus the acceleration of economic growth and the development of new techniques in production cannot be separated from the rise in population that had taken place in Germany since the middle of the eighteenth century. It provided the economy with an expanding market for new goods as well as with a cheap workforce. At the same time this population increase was intimately connected with growing productive resources and their use, if only by the fact that an expanding economy offers more people the chance to marry at an earlier age and thus increase the rate of demographic reproduction.

Within the borders of the future German nation-state the number of inhabitants rose from around 16–18 million in 1750 to some 24 million at the turn of the century, to 33 million in 1850, 41 million in 1871, and finally to 67 million on the eve of the First World War. Of course, there were differences in time and place. Annual growth rates, for example, oscillated between 0.72 per cent and 1.51 per cent for the period of 1871 to 1900; and before the foundation of the Empire the population of the Kingdom of Saxony grew by 34 per cent between 1850 and 1871, whereas Württemberg reached only 4 per cent.

Such differences were also due to increasing migration, especially from regions still dominated by agriculture to those where the new industries were demanding an increased workforce. As a rule, this resulted in a rapid growth of the urban population in Germany. Before 1850 there were four 'big cities' with 100,000 or more inhabitants:

Berlin (412,000), Hamburg 175,000), Breslau (110,000) and Munich (107,000); in 1871 Cologne, Dresden, Leipzig and Königsberg joined this number and the period of fastest growth still lay ahead, when the population of towns of the industrial areas like Dortmund, Bochum and Essen would grow between four- and sixfold within the time-span of a single generation. By 1914 two-thirds of the German people lived in towns and again two-thirds of these lived in the 'big cities' with more than 100,000 inhabitants.

As elsewhere in Europe, industrialization went together with demographic growth, migration and urbanization. And, as elsewhere, industrial revolution implied a revolution of the transport system as the essential part of the economic infrastructure of a modern expanding market. Between 1834 (when the first line between Nuremberg and Fürth in Bavaria was constructed), and 1873 the German rail network expanded to 24,000 miles; only the United States and Great Britain could surpass such a figure. And in the context of German industrialization the importance of the railways was not restricted to their role as a modern means of transport. As the biggest consumer of coal and steel they were at the centre of the closely interlocked heavy-industrial sectors, so that during the early stages of industrialization they were the most important area of investment because they offered the investor the prospect of quick and ample profit.

Thus, spearheaded by the railway a first industrial breakthrough occurred in the 1840s, but it was only with the end of political upheaval that the decisive period of economic development set in and the 1850s became the first boom period of a new capitalist market economy with a major industrial sector. Coal production in Prussia increased eightfold between 1849 and 1875, raw iron output fourteenfold, steel output fifty-fourfold; taken all together, the area of the German Customs Union became third among the industrial powers of Europe as a producer of iron and steel, surpassed only by Britain and France. At the same time new forms of technology were introduced; the number of steam-powered engines increased spectacularly and factory plants and mines grew in size. Alfred Krupp started his famous steel production in 1836 with just 60 employees. In 1873 he commanded a workforce of 16,000.

By the 1870s Germany had become one of the foremost European industrial nations. For a considerable time it had lagged behind the economic development of its western neighbours, especially Britain and France. This had partly been due to the political framework, to the fact that particularism implied a multitude of customs barriers, which stood in the way of the unfolding of a big national market as an essential precondition for economic modernization.

On the other hand, the latecomer could make short-cuts, could profit from the experiences and the results of the pioneers of the Industrial Revolution. For example, steel production in Germany could start on an advanced level because it made use of the Bessemer process, which had only been applied in England since 1856. Moreover, there existed closer links between the state and private capital than in the Anglo-Saxon countries; German chambers of commerce were not just associations of businessmen but semi-public institutions. And in 1860 the state railways totalled 5200 kilometres, private railways under government management 1400 and privately administered railways 4600 kilometres. But this did not imply undue interference in the mechanisms of a market economy. Even in the era of political reaction the German states pursued policies that favoured commerce and industrial development.

However, economic modernization exposed Germany to the vicissitudes of unfettered capitalism, in particular to the ups and downs of what was now becoming a world market. In 1873 the first boom collapsed and it was followed by the first 'Great Depression', which lasted until 1896. Overinvestment and overproduction led to industrial recession, deflation and unemployment. Yet, though the speed of growth and economic progress had been drastically reduced, another long-lasting phase of sustained growth between 1895 and 1913 gave Germany her first 'economic miracle'. On the eve of the First World War it had become a major economic world power. In most classical domains of industrial production like iron and steel it had overtaken Great Britain, and it was leading the world in new sophisticated fields of production like dyestuffs and electrical goods. 'Made in Germany' had become an international symbol for high quality.

Only then, at the beginning of the twentieth century, did the industrial sector begin to provide the largest part of German domestic product. It replaced agriculture, which until the closing decades of the nineteenth century had remained the backbone of economic development by providing food for a rapidly increasing population. Also, until the turn of the century, its share of the labour force was about 50 per cent. In order to offer a sufficient food supply for a growing urban population, new land was brought into cultivation and later on productivity was raised by the use of artificial fertilizers and the advent of mechanization in the form of threshing machines.

But whereas German industry was leading the world in many sectors at the turn of the century, agriculture, though in many ways also a success story, on the whole was in a precarious position and on the defensive. When it became clear that it was unable to feed the population of a modern urban-industrial state, Germany, in the 1870s, became an importer of grain. And when transport facilities in a world-wide market for foodstuff rapidly improved and prices fell accordingly, from 1879 onwards the powerful German agricultural lobby succeeded in putting pressure on the government to erect a wall of tariffs against competition, mainly from Russia and the United States. At the expense of the ordinary consumer, food prices were kept above world level for the benefit of middle and big agrarian producers, who had partly adapted to the mechanisms of a free-market society but who also tried to stem the tide of the expansion of world-wide free trade.

The thorough and often extremely rapid economic change Germany experienced during the second half of the nineteenth century had, of course, grave repercussions for the structure of German society, which can be summed up as the process of transition from a traditional corporate society to a modern class structure.

Before the impact of the demographic and industrial revolutions, a universally accepted hierarchy of rank and status had assigned a place for everyone: lord and peasant, master and journeyman, priest and professor. This order was broken up by accelerating movement in all spheres and in all directions: continuous and rising migration from the countryside into the cities, from one region to another or even as emigration to overseas countries or as immigration from Eastern Europe. But besides geographical, horizontal movement there was vertical rise and fall, up or down the social ladder.

Yet, despite the decline of the traditional corporate society and the emergence of new classes, like a rising bourgeoisie and a new prole-tarian working class, the German – and especially the Prussian – nobility still managed to retain their superior position at the top of the social hierarchy in many successful rearguard actions. Although they had lost substantial privileges, like their former special legal status which had been abolished in favour of general equality before the law, in Prussia they had clung to their right to entail their estates and to continue administering local justice as a kind of estate management. And though the Prussian Reform Edict of 1807 had entitled middle-class entrepreneurs to acquire landed estates, which usually formed the base of aristocratic power, in the early 1880s aristocrats who had successfully adapted to the rules and mechanisms of a market society still made up 68 per cent of the biggest landed proprietors.

Moreover, the real source of the influence the Prussian nobility still exerted stemmed from its strategic position within government and army. The second chamber of the Prussian parliament was predominantly aristocratic, and the Prussian gentry's privilege to enforce police regulation in the countryside and to appoint village mayors was not abolished until 1872. Until the collapse of the German Empire key positions not only in the army but also in the higher ranks of the administration were held by the nobility, which made up only 0.3 per cent of the German population. Contrary to the general trend of economic and social modernization with its final goal of a free-market society, the decades after the foundation of the German Empire witnessed a remarkable reinvigoration of the influence and power of the German nobility.

Those years also saw the formation of a powerful German bourgeoisie: the group of bankers, merchants, manufacturers and entrepreneurs who actually made the industrial revolution happen. Besides the huge fortunes amassed by those great magnates there was the growing wealth of a provincial middle class with its small-town capitalists and businessmen of diverse kinds. And alongside this propertied middle class were the members of Germany's educated middle class: lawyers and doctors and especially the great bulk of state officials like judges, administrators, professors and grammar school teachers – all of them with university degrees. Altogether, the members of this rising German middle class with its many internal divisions made up some 5 per cent of the whole population.

Quite a number of this new bourgeoisie had risen in life and were of unpretentious middle-class origin or even lower-class background. But whereas during the first half of the century a developing bourgeois identity had been most likely to define itself against the nobility, after the revolution the tendency grew to separate themselves from the lower classes: not only from the new factory proletariat, but even more so from the petty bourgeoisie. In the course of the late nineteenth century a distinctive lower middle class was taking shape: mainly craftsmen and small shopkeepers alongside the new white-collar employees like clerks, cashiers and overseers. Together this lower sector of the middle class accounted for around 12 per cent of the

German labour force between the 1870s and 1880s. Placed between the bourgeoisie and the working class, it was less a class in itself than a buffer zone, a social group which was fluid and transitional. And here it was mainly the artisans in the handicraft occupations who saw themselves confronted with the rising danger of being forced out of the production of goods which could now be provided much more cheaply by the new industries. Confined to a narrowing segment of the economy and faced by the decline of the handicraft trades and the decay of guild organizations, many artisans lost their former status, found their incomes squeezed below subsistence level and joined the great mass of 'lower orders' of German society.

About two-thirds of the German population lived below or at least near the poverty line. In the country these were the small peasants, the landless cottagers, who in some regions tried to make a living as weavers or spinners, the agricultural day-labourers and farm servants, many of them only recently released from feudal bondage. On the roads, besides numerous vagrants and pedlars, one would meet those who migrated seasonally in search of work. And in the towns there were the journeymen and the apprentices, the household servants, small shopkeepers and hawkers, prostitutes and beggars.

Within the urban sector of these 'lower orders' the rise of a new class provided the counterpoint to the formation of the entrepreneurial bourgeoisie: the new 'workers who sold their labour power to the factory or mine owner. This was the period when a true factory proletariat came into being, working to the rhythm of machines, subject to the division of labour, disciplined by factory clock and work regulations, supervised by foremen, remunerated by fixed wares or piece rates'.[1] Together with the growing number of former journeymen who, with the decline of the handicraft system, sank to the status of mere 'hands' in small workshops, these factory workers became the nucleus of a new German working class. It was slow in forming and expanding. In 1849 factory workers and miners made up 4.7 per cent of the Prussian workforce and this number rose to 6.8 per cent in 1861 until it reached 12 per cent at the time of the foundation of the empire. But after that the percentage of the urban wage-dependent working class in Germany rose steeply to more than 50 per cent of the whole workforce around the turn of the century.

Thus the traditional corporate society dominated by an agrarian economy had been replaced by a predominantly industrial urban society. This rapid fundamental change, which affected nearly all Germans irrespective of where they lived and how they lived, took place at the same time that, with the foundation of the Empire, a new political framework was being erected. Whereas in most European countries industrialization and the formation of the nation-state had occurred at different stages of their history, in Germany they happened simultaneously, which meant that two extremely difficult problems had to be solved at the same time. The belated German nation-state arose from complex conditions.

7

· · · · · · · ·

Prussia's Germany

Bismarck was not a German nationalist but a Prussian patriot. The aim of his policy was the extension and consolidation of Prussia and to this end he had to establish Prussian hegemony in Central Europe against Austria as his main rival. In 1866 and 1871 this was achieved by the foundation first of the *Norddeutscher Bund* and then of the *Deutsche Reich*. As it was based on the concept of the 'lesser Germany' solution of 1848, it was an 'unfinished national state' because it did not include all German-speaking people, especially not the German Austrians. Instead, it was in many respects a Greater Prussia. Prussia not only accounted for more than 50 per cent of the territory and population of Germany, but her dominant position was confirmed and further strengthened by the constitution of the *Reich* which, in its main parts, had been drafted by Bismarck himself.

CONSTITUTION AND POLITICAL CULTURE

In order to guarantee a maximum of continuity the new *Reich* again was a confederation of kingdoms, principalities and the three Hanseatic cities of Hamburg, Bremen and Lübeck. But behind this façade a much more centralized structure was erected, which kept Prussia unequivocally in control. Its central feature was a federal council (*Bundesrat*) of representatives from the individual states, where Prussia had an effective veto. Besides, the King of Prussia in his function as *Kaiser* was not only head of state and president of the federal council but also the supreme military commander of the *Reich*. He also appointed (and only he could dismiss) the *Reichskanzler* (Chancellor of the Empire as head of government), who would always be at the same time Prussian prime minister.

To balance these autocratic elements a parliament of the representatives of the people (*Reichstag*) shared legislation with the *Bundesrat*. The composition of this assembly was based on universal manhood suffrage, because Bismarck, from his experiences with his Prussian peasants during the revolution of 1848, was convinced of the fundamentally conservative disposition of the majority of the common people.

However, the real power of this parliament was limited. It could neither control the executive, nor did its power of the budget fully

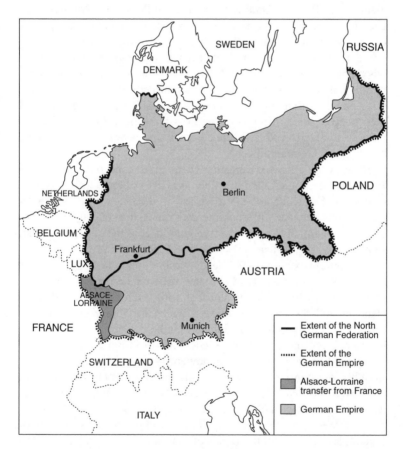

Map 6 Prussia's Germany, 1871–1918 (adapted from Dietrich Orlow, *A History of Modern Germany, 1971 to the Present* (Englewood Cliffs, NJ, 1987), p. 32).

extend to military affairs. And though the chancellor was 'accountable' to parliament, this only meant that he would have to defend his policies on the stage of the *Reichstag*; it did not imply that he was responsible to and removable by parliamentary majority. Moreover, the budget for military and naval expenditures was fixed for several years at a time and linked to the size of the army.

Prussia's dominant position within the German Empire was not restricted to the hard facts of the constitutional framework. Political culture and the political and social mentality of those who set the tone in German society was also heavily influenced by the key elements of Prussian tradition. The main pillar of the Prussian state had always been her oversized army, which had won all the victories on the road to unification, so after 1871 this army was to shape society to a considerable extent. Not only was its presence visible everywhere, its officers also provided the key role models for the upper middle classes where members of the bourgeoisie, especially academics and professionals, by adopting the habit of duelling adapted their code of honour to that of the Prussian officer. Order and discipline were understood to be the cardinal virtues not only of soldiers, but of every German citizen.

Besides the army the bureaucracy, as the second pillar of the old Prussian state, represented the other hard core of the political system of the new German empire. Particularly in the face of growing internal tensions between different interest groups, the state and its representatives claimed to act as the true guardians of the general interest, standing above political and social conflicts.

To a certain extent Prussia's leading role stood in the way of a rapid and smooth consolidation of the new nation-state. In the first place there were Austria's former allies of 1866 such as the kingdom of Hanover and the city of Frankfurt, which had been annexed after Prussia's victory. Others, mainly in southern Germany, would still have preferred the old German Federation to Prussian hegemony, as did most Catholics, who from now on were a religious minority (roughly one-third of the population) under a Protestant monarch. Moreover, the *Reich* contained substantial national minorities within its borders: the largest of these, and of longest standing, were the Poles in the eastern provinces, mostly former victims of the partitions of Poland; and after 1866 the Danes of Schleswig-Holstein had become German subjects as had the inhabitants of Alsace-Lorraine after 1871. And though the Empire was Prussia's Germany, at the same time many influential Prussian conservatives, headed by their king, had grave misgivings about Bismarck's pact with German nationalism and feared that Prussian identity might dissolve and be lost in the broader context of a German nation.

POLITICAL MODERNIZATION

In fact, the foundation of the German Empire did not mark the climax but rather the starting point of unification. The great tasks for the future were to achieve a genuinely unified nation-state and to move forward on the road towards some kind of democratic parliamentary system in order to close the gap between economic and political modernization. The chief instrument of progress in both sectors was the German parliament: the *Reichstag*.

In spite of the fact that there had not been established a parliamentary system which would bind the government to the assent of the majority in parliament, the *Reichstag* soon gained in status and became an important centre of political interest and activity – the stage where national unity came to life and which served as a counterpoint to the domineering position of the King of Prussia as *Kaiser*. The reasons for this were parliament's decisive role in legislation and the fact that it served as the main theatre for public debate and thus as a focal point of public opinion. The popular legitimacy it acquired rested on the fact that it was elected by the most democratic franchise in Europe: free, direct and equal for males over the age of 25, which made the *Reichstag* a genuine national representation. And the rising number of voters at general elections (from 51 per cent in 1871 to 84.9 per cent in 1912), which took place every five years, clearly indicated a growing trend towards democracy.

At the same time the *Reich* was a state whose administration respected and guaranteed the rule of law as well as personal freedom. Moreover, the general trend of legislation throughout the years went in the direction of the consolidation and extension of civil rights, including freedom of the press and the right to strike for workers. And there was a bulk of new fiscal, commercial, legal and social legislation as an important factor of further national integration. It culminated in the implementation of a new Civil Code in 1900, which is still in force at the present day. Moreover, a single currency, common weights and measures, the unification and nationalization of the railways and the establishment of an imperial civil service contributed to making the Empire more centralized. Political reality began to diverge from the original constitutional concept of just another German Federation; Germany was on the way towards being a compact nation-state where overarching political unity is not only the subject of national enthusiasm but a hard fact of everyday life.

In another domain, in the field of social policy, the German Empire was even in the van of political progress. During the 1880s Bismarck introduced a number of insurance schemes, based on the principles of universal coverage, compulsory participation, income-related contributions and centralized administration, which were aimed at creating a healthier and more satisfied workforce. On the eve of the First World War, more than 15 million Germans were covered by health insurance, 28 million insured against accidents and one million were receiving regular pensions. This system of state provision even served as a model for British liberals like Lloyd George and Winston Churchill.

A further important factor of political modernization was the formation of a German party system, testifying to the emergence of remarkably vigorous popular politics. Here, roots go back to the German revolution of 1848 where the National Assembly had been divided into conservatives, radical democrats and a liberal majority composed of different sections. After their defeat by the counter-revolution the democrats were reduced to a mere regional political force in southern Germany, mainly in Württemberg, and by the 1870s there were four major political camps. Liberals, conservatives, socialists and Catholics formed the main elements of a party system that was to persist through to 1918 and in some parts until the dissolution of the Weimar Republic in the 1930s.

In the aftermath of 1866 the liberals had split into a National-Liberal majority, which supported Bismarck's policy of unification and was ready to collaborate with his government, and left-wing liberals – partly former democrats – the Progressive Party, which in 1884 together with a number of 'Secessionists' from the National-Liberals formed the *Deutsche Freisinnige Partei*. In 1870, the year of the proclamation of the doctrine of papal infallibility by the Vatican Council, the German Centre Party was founded by Catholics and other minorities who felt threatened by a Protestant/Prussian-dominated unification. In 1875 the Social Democratic Party (SPD) was the result of a merger of two working-class parties founded in the 1860s by Ferdinand Lasalle and August

Bebel. And in the following year the formation of the German Conservative Party marked the belated assent of conservatives (who had severely criticized nationalist tendencies) to Bismarck's policy of unification. Throughout the period of the Empire this party would be dominated by the agrarian interests of the Prussian nobility.

This four-party arrangement (plus small nationalist minority parties of Alsatians, Poles and Danes and new anti-Semitic organizations in the 1890s) did not change during the whole period, but within this framework the fortunes of the different parties varied considerably and their general character changed fundamentally.

With the rising importance of the role of parliament and a growing turnout at the polls the political styles and organizations of the parties were transformed. Here the SPD served as the model of what a modern mass party should be like: oratory not just inside the chamber but also 'out of doors'; voting discipline of the parliamentary party; paid officials for the party machine and party newspapers. Even among Liberals and Conservatives the gentleman-politician was gradually replaced by the hard-working professional and committee expert.

In the period of time between the foundation of the *Reich* and the outbreak of the First World War the strength of the parties changed considerably. Only the Catholic Centre Party was hardly affected by ups and downs at the polls; in 1874 it won 22.9 per cent of the seats in the *Reichstag*; in the following elections this number rose to between 24 per cent and 26 per cent and in 1912 it was down to 22.8 per cent again. Otherwise a dramatic U-turn had been effected with regard to the party composition of the *Reichstag*. In 1871 National-Liberals and Conservatives, who together supported Bismarck's government, had secured 60.3 per cent of the votes, which gave them more than 62 per cent of the seats in the *Reichstag*. At the elections of 1912 those numbers were down to 26.3 per cent and 25.6 per cent. These dramatic losses corresponded to spectacular gains by the opposition parties, especially the SPD. In 1871, the two workers' parties had gained just 3.1 per cent of the votes; after their merger they got nearly 9.1 per cent in 1877 and in 1912 they won 34.8 per cent, which gave them 110 seats and made them the strongest parliamentary party.

Thus parliamentary politics of the Empire culminated in the paradoxical situation whereby those parties which once had been branded as enemies of the *Reich* by Bismarck commanded a permanent majority of the seats in the *Reichstag* after 1890: the left-wing liberals, the Catholics and the socialists.

Since his appointment to office in Prussia Bismarck, a staunch defender of the royal prerogative, had always fought those liberals who aimed at the introduction of parliamentary government. And, vice versa, the radical liberals had only once been willing to support Bismarck's policy, i.e. in his fight against the Catholic Church during the so-called *Kulturkampf* (struggle of civilizations) in the 1870s.

Partly from tactical reasons – i.e. to strengthen his alliance with the National-Liberals and also as a preventive move against the formidable political wing of the Catholic minority, the Centre Party – as well as from his fundamental belief in the untrammelled sovereignty of the state, Bismarck went onto the offensive and began to abolish or at least reduce long-established rights and privileges of the Catholic Church. This serious conflict between State and Church led to the expulsion of the Jesuits from the *Reich*, the attempt to establish state control not only over education but also over the appointment of the clergy and it culminated in a bundle of punitive legislation authorizing the seizure of Church property and the expulsion and even imprisonment of some members of the Church.

Soon enthusiastic liberals outdid Bismarck on the German front of this Europe-wide fight for 'progress' and against Catholic 'backwardness', but they, as well as the chancellor, had underestimated the stubborn passive resistance of the German Catholics, and in the end both sides were locked in stalemate. After the death of the militant Pope Pius IX in 1878 the struggle was slowly wound up in a number of compromises.

The intensity of this *Kulturkampf* had been part of the heritage of the age of Reformation and Counter-Reformation, which had left the old German Empire as a biconfessional state. Now one of the powerful legacies of this renewed conflict was a long-lasting gulf between a Catholic 'ghetto' and a world shaped by the tenets of modern Protestant liberalism and led by the professsional and business classes. And from now on Catholics would accept the new Germany even more slowly. The second important legacy of the *Kulturkampf* was that it had helped to consolidate the position of the Centre Party as a strong parliamentary minority – an erratic bloc in the landscape of political parties, which would always stand in the way of clear majorities either on the left or on the right wing of the *Reichstag*.

The winding up of the *Kulturkampf* had been hastened by the beginning of an attack on another outsider group in Bismarck's Germany: the organized German working class. Earlier than elsewhere in Europe workers in Germany, in the wake of the Industrial Revolution, formed their own political organizations, which proclaimed democracy and social justice as their primary aim. Since they had been critical of Germany's unification from above, and because in their programme of May 1875 they claimed to 'aspire with all legal means a free state and a socialist society', and August Bebel (one of the founding fathers of the SPD) in 1871 had hailed the Paris Commune as the great example to be followed, the party soon became an object of fear and suspicion for ruling conservative and liberal elites. Acting out of a mixture of party politics and genuine conviction as to the danger of a socialist revolution, Bismarck used two assassination attempts on Kaiser Wilhelm as a pretext for his Socialist Law of 1878, which outlawed the party organization and the socialist press. It was followed by a campaign of persecution and repression, and in the course of the next 12 years about 1500 people were imprisoned and many driven into exile.

But in the end this law against the Socialists proved as counterproductive as the laws against the Catholics. In order not to violate the constitution one loophole had to be left: social democrats were still allowed to stand for parliamentary elections. And though election campaigning suffered from the provisions of the law, the SPD more than doubled their votes between 1878 and 1890 by means of the ballot, and the number of their seats rose from 9 to 35. When the ban was lifted in 1890 the party still had 100,000 members and this number rose to some 720,000 in 1910, making the SPD by far the biggest Socialist Party in Europe.

But despite this success story, as in the case of the Catholics, repression left a dubious legacy for the political culture in Germany. Like the Catholics the Social Democrats were labelled 'enemies of the Empire' and the experience of being outlawed created bitterness and alienation and at the same time reinforced solidarity among the members of the workers' movement who were now even more firmly convinced of the necessity of the coming of the revolution Marx had predicted. Moreover, since Bismarck had stigmatized Socialists and Catholics as 'enemies of the Empire' it became a special trait of German parliamentary politics often to enlarge the gulf between government and opposition by transforming political differences into irreconcilable antagonisms.

This development was reinforced by the general trend in German party politics to develop and maintain strong ideological positions. As the constitution did not provide for the formation of parliamentary governments, the parties, unrestrained by the need to exercise political responsibility, had no opportunity to experience the benefits of political pragmatism and rather stuck to 'politics of principle', so that mental barriers between parties like the SPD and the Centre became a serious impediment to parliamentary co-operation. In the end, German party politics resulted in the paradox that those political minorities which once had been stigmatized as 'enemies of the Empire' collectively represented the majority of the German electorate; however, the structure of the constitution and strong class antagonisms made it nearly impossible for the true majority to assert itself.

On the whole, during the first two decades after its foundation, Prussia's Germany was a political system which, instead of being nicely balanced, was under continuous strains and stresses because it was torn by a number of opposing and contradictory forces and movements. On the one hand, Germany obviously was advancing on the road towards national unity and democracy. On the other hand, the rise of the political parties and of popular identification with political issues was contributing to a growing pressure on the constitution, which seemed on the brink of giving way to a parliamentary system.

Yet there were limits to these changes. In spite of its growing influence the *Reichstag* ultimately remained without decisive power because the central pillars of the Prusso-German constitution remained untouched, including the prerogatives of the *Kaiser* who, with the accession to the throne of Wilhelm II in 1888, aspired to assume a leading role in politics by establishing his own 'personal rule'. And the greatest barrier on the road to political modernization remained Prussia with its notorious three-class franchise of 1849.

In order to stem the tide of democracy the Prussian electorate had been divided into three groups according to wealth, each electing the same number of delegates. This meant that the electors of the wealthy minority classes 1 and 2 had twice as much influence on the composition of the lower house of the Prussian parliament as the three-quarters or more of the population relegated to the third class of voters. Originally this franchise had been designed to guarantee conservative majorities but in fact, as it favoured the well-to-do voters, soon the liberal parties profited from it. In any case it denied electoral success to the SPD which, though it got 18.7 per cent of the votes in 1903, did not win a single seat in the Prussian chamber of deputies and in 1913 needed 796,000 votes to gain only ten. The fact that politics in Prussia were out of step with politics at national level considerably added to the tensions and divides, which were the stuff of German politics at the turn of the century.

Besides what might be called the 'Prussia problem', there was what might be called the 'Bismarck problem'. As the architect of the German nation-state, who had established this new German *Reich* as one of the leading powers of Europe, he remained the dominant figure of German politics not just until his dismissal from office in 1890, but as a focal point for disgruntled conservatives and nationalists until his death in 1898. With his public scorn of parties and parliaments he cast a long shadow on German political culture, especially on parts of the German middle class, which made hero-worship of the strong man and the call for politics 'above the parties' the essentials of their political agenda.

Thus German society in general and German politics in particular were under continuous pressure as the result of many and various divisions and growing tensions between the interests of different groups. This did not just imply a clash of classes, the antagonism between the rich and the poor, between aristocracy, bourgeoisie and working class, but also between agrarian and industrial interests, between Protestants and Catholics, between Prussians and Bavarians, between white-collar and blue-collar workers, between the stifling conventions of official culture and a new cultural avant-garde; interest groups and lobbying were nowhere else so widely found as in Germany.

Many of these tensions were the result of clashes between accelerating modernization and the forces of traditionalism and were common to most European societies. But contrasts were often sharper in Germany, which was partly due to the fact that it had only recently been forged into a nation-state. On the other hand, those divisive forces were at least partly counterbalanced by the unifying force of nationalism. But this was a new nationalism which had undergone a change in its aims and its character.

NATIONALISM IN THE AGE OF IMPERIALISM

Before unification German nationalism had mainly rested on a highly valued common cultural tradition and though it had also been shaped by antagonism towards other nations, especially the French as the traditional sworn enemy, its chief political aim had been national union and therefore particularism and princely despotism had been targeted as its main obstacles – before 1871 German nationalism had concentrated on Germany.

After the achievement of 1871 German nationalism lost its revolutionary quality because it no longer meant opposition to the status quo. From now on it was resolved to defend the new status quo; within the political spectrum it had changed sides from the 'left' to the 'right' because now its former enemies – such as governments, even princes and large parts of the Prussian Conservatives – proclaimed national aims and ideas. At the same time German nationalism turned its attention to Germany's place among the other nations. And whereas during its early stages it had often been affected by the experience of defeat and humiliation – what could be called the 'Thirty Years' War syndrome' – national pride could now bask in the triumph of three victorious wars won by the Prussian army. This new patriotism, the general sense of being a member of a powerful and respected nation, flourished in the course of the years and was much stronger on the eve of the First World War than it had been in 1870; and though initially the Protestant middle classes had been the driving force behind this nationalism, now even Social Democrats would have liked to demonstrate that they, too, were good Germans, if only a repressive ruling class would let them and no longer defame them as 'unpatriotic rabble'. More than 700 monuments – towers and pillars and statues – were erected after Bismarck's death by various civil societies and associations to honour the founding father of the German nation-state.

But as elsewhere in Europe, at the end of the nineteenth century, which marked the climax of the European nation-state, there was more than simple national pride to this new nationalism. This was also the age of imperialism, of heightened competition between the European powers opening up a race to carve out colonial possessions for themselves. Therefore fear was growing among German nationalists that Germany might be blocked by rival powers like Britain and France from getting her 'place in the sun' in the imperial sphere. New nationalistic organizations like the Pan-German League (founded 1891), the Society for Germandom Abroad (1881), the Colonial Society (1887), the German Navy League (1898) which even became a mass organization), and many more put pressure on or were used by certain political groups to put that pressure on German governments to assert global German interests. To this end they also proclaimed German cultural superiority over all other nations, a global 'German Mission'.

This new nationalistic turn of German foreign policy soon put an end to Bismarck's achievements in the realm of foreign policy, by which he had succeeded in safeguarding the new Germany's precarious position among the European powers. He had been aware of the danger of unbalancing the long-established Concert of Powers when a powerful state like the German *Reich* was placed in the centre of Europe, and for the rest of his life had been haunted by a '*cauchemar des coalitions*', by the nightmare of a coalition of the old powers against the newcomer. Therefore, as soon as the Empire had been founded, Bismarck did not tire of openly asserting that there would be no further claims for future expansion. After 1871, in foreign affairs he had strategically become a supporter of the European status quo. Realizing that France would always be bent on revenge, in the course of the years following the foundation of the *Reich* he spun a complex network of alliances with consummate diplomatic skill to ensure that France would be unable to form any coalition against the *Reich*. The heart of this system was the Dual Alliance (1879) with Prussia's former rival, the Habsburg Empire, which even echoed the Greater German Concept of the '48 Revolution'. Italy joined this alliance in 1882 and even Russia, in spite of her continuous rivalry with Austria, was added to Bismarck's system in 1887. All this was achieved by a cool, calculating cabinet policy, but this achievement soon turned out to be precarious in an age when popular pressures and ideologies were of increasing importance.

Bismarck had been forced to make concessions when he gave in to demands for German overseas expansion and opened up the way for the foundation of German colonies in Africa and among the Pacific Islands. And when he was forced to resign from office in 1890 because William II was resolved to pursue his own course in politics, the new, harsher kind of nationalism soon gained ground in the field of German foreign policy. When William's third chancellor, Count Bülow, officially gave up the preservation of the status quo as the supreme goal of Germany's foreign policy and claimed 'a place in the sun' instead, Germany's role became more aggressive and it was particularly the meddlesome and hyperactive style of her foreign policy which provoked universal distrust. The most familiar example of this new turn was the German challenge to British naval power when, from 1898 onwards, Admiral Tirpitz as Secretary of State for the Navy was allowed to push on with battleship building on a grand scale in order to establish his country among the great naval powers. So Germany now took part in a general arms race, which was the result of a general growing imperialist tension. And it remains open to dispute if even Bismarck could have succeeded in preserving his alliance system under the conditions of the new era, when old-style cabinet diplomacy faltered under the pressures of public opinion and when nationalism deteriorated into chauvinism.

After the turn of the century Bismarck's nightmares came true. In 1904 Britain and France, who had fought so many wars against each other, formed the Entente Cordiale, which settled unanswered questions between the two countries, and thus made way for a closer co-operation even in times of war. And when two years later London agreed on a similar arrangement with Russia, the *Reich* and Austria were isolated, the encirclement was complete and a future war was likely to be fought on two fronts.

This did not keep the German military establishment from preparing for a 'preventive war' by means of the Schlieffen Plan (named after the Chief of Staff, General Alfred Schlieffen), which foresaw a quick decisive strike on Paris before turning against a Russian invasion in the east. But as this included a violation of Belgian neutrality, it also implied a further challenge to Britain, which had never tolerated a major continental power controlling the opposite coastline.

Plans and preparations like these went together with a palpable sense of crisis all over Europe and a general mounting fatalism about the inevitability of war. Whilst all the Powers professed a desire for peace, all were preparing for war. And there was a widespread feeling among Europeans that war would have a liberating and cleansing effect and would in fact show the way out of permanent inner crisis.

At the same time the temperature of international relations rose, especially through repeated regional wars fought in the Balkans, until the assassination of the heir to the Habsburg throne by Serb nationalists on 28 June 1914 triggered a fateful chain reaction leading up to the first global war, which was to be remembered as the Great War – a watershed to a new age in general and to a new period of German history in particular.

Though Germany had had her share in the general build-up to war and had also substantially contributed to the actual outbreak by her unconditional support for Austria, during the first days of August the government succeeded in its presentation of the conflict as a defensive war against the expansionist policy of autocratic Russia. And, indeed, when the *Kaiser* declared on 4 August: 'I no longer know any parties

– I just know Germans', this statement was in tune with widespread enthusiasm among the general public, and even most members of the SPD voted for the war credits.

However, hopes for quick victory were soon disappointed when gallant charges were stopped by elaborate systems of sandbagged trenches, and new weapons of destruction led to new forms of carnage in a gruesome war of attrition with huge losses on all sides; Germany alone counted 1.73 million killed. At the same time, war for the Germans turned into a total war which strongly affected the civilian population because British control of the sea had a devastating effect on food supply: starvation was responsible for 750,000 deaths during the war.

At the same time domestic politics deteriorated. The *Reichstag* could not play a major role, the *Kaiser* was not up to the leading role assigned to him by the constitution and soon was reduced to a mere figurehead. In his place the Supreme Military Command began to emerge as the arbiter of German politics and in 1917–18 the country was ruled by the *de facto* military dictatorship of Generals Hindenburg and Ludendorff. While by 1917 a majority of the *Reichstag* supported a 'Resolution for Peace without Annexations' as the first move for a general peace, the military command went on pursuing far-reaching war aims which were to secure a German-dominated Central Europe.

When in the winter of 1918 the Bolshevik Revolution forced Russia to agree to a separate peace at Brest-Litovsk, it had to hand over the Baltic states and Poland and had to grant independence to the Ukraine and Finland. However, ultimate defeat was inevitable when, after the USA had entered the war on the Allied side and a final German effort on the Western Front had failed, parliamentary government was finally introduced on the initiative of the military command in order to agree to a capitulation so severe that the victorious Allies could dictate the terms of peace. At the same time, the imperial fleet mutinied in the ports of Kiel and Wilhelmshaven; socialist revolution broke out in Munich and Berlin; William II fled to the Netherlands; Germany threatened to sink into chaos. By November 1918 the short history of the *Kaiserreich,* of Prussia's Germany, was over.

8

....

Weimar Germany

The modern German Empire had lasted for less than half a century; the first German democracy collapsed after only 14 years. The history of this period will therefore concentrate on the causes of its downfall.

THE UNFINISHED REVOLUTION

Though it was not necessarily doomed from the start, the turbulent beginnings of German democracy were always overshadowed by defeat and humiliation, and as it developed it was not only burdened with problems stemming from the past but it also had to tackle huge difficulties arising in the future course of events.

There would not have been a change in government without the looming disaster of military defeat in the autumn of 1918. When the supreme military commanders, Hindenburg and Ludendorff, realized that they could not possibly win the war, the generals thought it advisable to hand over more power to a new civilian government with Prince Max von Baden as chancellor. Now, in a rush, ministerial responsibility to parliament, the control of the armed forces by civilian government and the abolition of the Prussian three-class franchise were introduced. Since Emperor William II refused to assume any further responsibility and by his abdication made way for the declaration of a German Republic on 9 November, a decisive progressive move had been made in the eyes of those who wanted to turn Germany into a modern democracy.

Two days later a member of the Centre Party, Matthias Erzberger, signed a treaty of armistice because Hindenburg and Ludendorff had put pressure on the *Reichstag*, which was dominated by Social

Democrats and the Centre Party, to negotiate an armistice on an emergency basis. They had pressed for the transition to parliamentary democracy because the American President Woodrow Wilson had signalled that in any negotiations for peace he would prefer as a partner a German government that was based on broader general consent than the present rulers of Germany. But while they urged the new civilian government to agree to a speedy armistice at any price, the German army, victorious in the east, was still intact on the Western Front and had nowhere been driven back onto German territory.

This gave the Supreme Command the opportunity to circulate the rumour of a 'stab in the back' of an otherwise undefeated army which had been betrayed by Bolsheviks and Jews at home. From this blunt lie grew a long-term political myth which had disastrous consequences for the young republic, because the myth seemed to be confirmed by the fact that revolution broke out at the same time.

Sparked off by a sailors' mutiny within the Imperial Fleet and spurred on by the example of the Bolshevik Revolution in Russia, radical sailors', soldiers' and workers' councils were formed in many places and began to wrest control from local government institutions. Such moves were supported by the radical wing of German Socialists, the so-called Independent Social Democratic Party (USPD) and the Spartacus League which soon was to form the nucleus of the German Communist Party (KPD). Their political aim was the foundation of a socialist republic based on a general nationalization of the means of production. In January 1919 an unbridgeable gulf opened between moderate Social Democrats who stood up for parliamentary democracy and the radical left propagating the Bolshevik model of government by people's councils.

The political situation in Germany at the end of the war can be compared to a triangle. One side was formed by the pillars of the old regime: the army – still in parts an intact fighting force – and the civil service; the second side was the old parliamentary majority of Social Democrats, Centre Party and Liberals from the Left, all aiming at the establishment of democracy and parliamentary government; on the third side were those who were in favour of an immediate and thorough socialist revolution.

In the first stage of the ensuing struggle for power the moderates of the middle way won the day: the SPD under the leadership of Friedrich Ebert, and its allies. But they won at a high price, because when during the turbulent weeks between 9 November 1918 and the middle of

January 1919 Germany was on the brink of chaos, with demonstrations, strikes, street-fighting and barricades in many places, the Social Democratic leaders accepted the support of the army in their effort to maintain law and order.

This deal left the second German Revolution incomplete, i.e. it remained restricted to the sphere of politics, especially to its constitutional framework. And the advocates of revolution, the radical Left, were repeatedly repressed and lost their prominent leaders Rosa Luxemburg and Karl Liebknecht, who were brutally murdered by soldiers called in to suppress a spontaneous uprising in Berlin in January 1919. On the other hand, the army, the judiciary and the civil service were to remain largely untouched by change – with grave consequences for the future of the Republic.

The SPD and their leader Ebert have often been severely criticized for having betrayed the revolution as the ultimate aim of socialist policy and for having offered the conservative forces the chance to regroup and regain confidence after having been thrown into disarray by the immediate threat of revolution. But Ebert feared that a successful socialist revolution in Germany might provoke the Western Allies to invade Germany. He was also firmly convinced of the necessity to turn Germany into a parliamentary democracy in order to avoid further chaos and achieve political stability. In his opinion only a parliamentary government could provide a framework for co-operation with members of moderate parties and thus a stable basis for further economic and social reforms.

To this end, a caretaker government organized general elections for a National Assembly which was to lay down a constitution for the new German Republic. This constituent parliament – in a way, forerunner to the Frankfurt *Paulskirche* of 1948 – was to convene in Weimar in order to be far enough away from unruly Berlin and at the same time to invoke the spirit of the great poets Goethe and Schiller who, more than a century ago, had made Weimar the capital of 'another Germany', a Germany of peaceful cultural superiority. On 19 January 1919 the most democratic election in German history so far was held with all men and women over 20 years eligible to vote.

Although the SPD led all other parties with 11.5 million votes and 163 seats, they were disappointed because they had hoped for an absolute majority. Having gained 38 per cent – which followed the trend of the last elections for the *Reichstag* when the Social Democrats had at last achieved 34 per cent – they were forced to form a coalition government with the Centre Party (6 million votes; 89 seats) and the German Democratic Party (DDP, 5.5 million; 75 seats) as a new organization of the old liberal Left. Together the three commanded a majority of 76.1 per cent of the votes, which gave them a broad and firm basis for the drafting of the constitution as well as for the first democratic government, to be led by the SPD. Yet, this coalition of democrats was soon to lose its majority. When the next general election was held under the new constitution on 6 June 1920, it suffered dramatic losses: the SPD's share fell from 37.9 per cent to 21.7 per cent, the DDP's to 8.2 per cent and the Centre dropped moderately to 13.6 per cent, while the big winners were the parties on the extreme right and left.

This result marked a decisive turn in the general trend for, from now on until the collapse of the Weimar Republic, the coalition of democrats was never again to gain a majority at general elections. The true reason for the failure of democracy in Germany at the beginning of the twentieth century was the paradox that as soon as democracy was established, the number of democrats ready to make it work, and to defend it, rapidly dwindled. In the end, a substantial majority in parliament voted for the abolition of democracy and in favour of Hitler's dictatorship. But this does not imply that from its very beginning democracy was doomed to failure – the ultimate dissolution of the Republic was due to various causes and circumstances. Among other factors the new German constitution has often been criticized for certain weaknesses that later facilitated the final collapse.

THE CONSTITUTION

This constitution, drafted by a group of liberal experts under the leadership of the eminent lawyer Hugo Preuss, attempted to combine the essentials of European parliamentary democracy with the characteristic features of the American presidential system. It defined Germany as a federal republic where the central power and national law took precedence over the *Länder* (the member states), and with a president as head of state who was to be elected by the people every seven years. This president, who as head of state replaced the hereditary office of the *Kaiser*, was given far-reaching personal power. He possessed the right to nominate and dismiss Chancellors, to dissolve parliament and call new elections and to appoint public officials. In times of emergency he could even assume temporary dictatorial power.

On the other hand, the constitution stressed the tenets of democracy. The electoral system was based on the principle of proportional representation so that all parties above a certain low threshold obtained seats in the *Reichstag* – a system which contributed to the proliferation of parties during the years and rendered the formation and the stability of coalition governments increasingly difficult (altogether, in the period between February 1919 and January 1933, twenty-one different cabinets came to power). Parliament was to be elected at least every four years by the vote of all men and women over the age of twenty. Moreover, the constitution introduced certain elements of direct democracy: on major policy issues referenda could be held.

All in all, this was a very progressive constitution because it provided a broad range of civil liberties – guaranteeing equality for women, among other things – and it also contained provisions designed to promote social justice. But as it turned out, this was a constitution designed for steady politics in peaceful times rather than for a situation of permanent crisis which more or less dominated the era of Weimar Germany. In the end it offered loopholes to those who aimed at the liquidation of democracy; it did not cause the fall of the Republic but it was instrumental in bringing about its destruction.

THE TREATY OF VERSAILLES

Before the National Assembly assented to the new constituton, the new government had to sign another document, which would remain an issue of utmost importance until the end of the Republic: the Peace Treaty of Versailles between the victorious powers and defeated Germany. When its provisions were finally revealed in early summer 1919 they proved to be extremely harsh, particularly as the German government had not been allowed to participate in the negotiations of the great Peace Conference, which was organized as a congress of victors.

The German Chancellor, the Social Democrat Philipp Scheidemann, declared such an imposed settlement, which later was to be called a *Diktat,* to be unacceptable and he and his cabinet resigned. But as military leaders made it clear that Germany was in no position to resume a war which would finally lead to the complete disintegration of the German nation-state, a new government, also led by the SPD, had to sign the Treaty on 28 June 1919.

Under its provisions Germany lost all her colonies. Alsace-Lorraine was to be returned to France, and the Saar basin on the western border was internationalized for 15 years – France would enjoy the profits of the rich coal production of this region. In the east, parts of Prussian territory were restored to a newly reconstituted Poland, which was also given a 'Corridor' to the Baltic, which separated East Prussia from the rest of Germany. Moreover, there was never to be a union with Austria. In order to eliminate any future threat from German military power, the army was to be reduced to 100,000 men, a reduced navy was to have no submarines, no air force would be permitted and border areas were to be demilitarized.

But the greatest irritant for the future was the notorious Article 231 of the treaty, the war guilt clause: 'The Allies and Associated Governments affirm and Germany accepts the responsibility of Germany and her allies for causing all the damage to which the Allied and Associated Governments and their nationals have been subjected as a consequence of the war imposed upon them by the aggression of Germany and her allies.' In consequence of this responsibility Germany was to pay reparations – their total amount to be determined later. The details for the payment of the enormous sum of 226 billion marks were announced two years later, and as well as the immediate economic repercussions, a huge wave of indignation was unleashed among Germans. Throughout the short history of the Weimar Republic negotiations as to the definite amount and the length and the modes of payment of these reparations were almost continuously on the political agenda.

Thus, the collective trauma of the Thirty Years' War recurred on the occasion of a peace conference which again disposed of Germany's future in a way that caused the majority of Germans to feel humiliated and victimized all over again. For after a war which – as they saw it – had been forced on them, now the victorious enemies ruthlessly and systematically endeavoured to emasculate Germany by minimizing her military strength, reducing her territory and ruining her economy beyond recovery, while at the same time stigmatizing the Germans as the sole culprits.

Growing resentment spurred growing revisionism. It soon became obvious that the treaty's main weakness was that it was too harsh and too mild at the same time. Lenient, in so far as the majority of the

Map 7 Weimar Germany (adapted from Dietrich Orlow, *A History of Modern Germany, 1971 to the Present* (Englewood Cliffs, NJ, 1987), p. 143).

Allied Powers had declined to take up the proposals of the French generals for a thorough liquidation of the German nation-state by, for example, creating a separate Bavaria and breaking away the Rhineland. Instead, even under the provisions of the treaty Germany remained a large and populous nation, with enough breathing space to utter her protest against these otherwise harsh conditions and with enough strength left to attempt to evade or at least to alter the peace terms imposed on her.

Foremost among the negative consequences of the Treaty of Versailles for German politics was that many of those who opposed it linked it to the myth of the 'stab in the back', which had gained considerable currency since the summer of 1919. The 'traitors of November 1919', they argued, were the same men who had set up and supported republic and democracy and who now had put their signatures to the Treaty of Versailles and even took the first steps to comply with its political and economic provisions. The widespread, persistent and energetic fight of many groups and individuals against the *Diktat* in many cases became a fight against democracy at home.

Soon the Republic was subjected to onslaughts from various sides and the following years were characterized by attempts at coup d'états and revolts, by demonstrations and strikes and a general atmosphere of ongoing vituperation against the democratic government, which culminated in a number of political assassinations; not only did prominent members of the Left like Liebknecht, Rosa Luxemburg and the head of a revolutionary government in Munich, Kurt Eisner, fall victim to fanatical members of the radical Right, but also Matthias Erzberger and Walther Rathenau, two prominent politicians who had done much to help Germany recover from her defeat but who had been defamed as 'November criminals' and 'appeasement politicians'.

INFLATION AND THE GREAT DEPRESSION

Political crisis was exacerbated by severe economic difficulties which, as has sometimes been argued, in the long run were the chief cause for the collapse of the Weimar Republic. To start with there was a catastrophic inflation with its extraordinary climax in 1923. Its roots lay in the earlier choice of financing the war exclusively through borrowing. This had seemed to German politicians to be the most politically expedient method. Instead of increasing taxes, which would have been a sound approach from the financial point of view, Germany's national debt rose from a modest 300 million marks on the eve of the war to a massive 51 billion 200 million by its end. At the same time the currency had been inflated from 6.6 billion marks in circulation in 1913 to 33.1 billion by 1918.

This burden was increased by all the consequences of defeat: industrial production was almost halved and when, at the same time, the government was faced with the enormous task of reintegrating 10 million soldiers into the economy, apart from the many invalids who had to receive modest pensions, the number of the unemployed rose sharply. And finally, of course, the payment of reparations had to be met.

When the government began trying to meet these excessive and constantly rising demands by printing more and more paper money, the value of the currency spiralled totally out of control. In 1923 a state of hyperinflation was reached; on 9 June that year at a Berlin market one egg was 800 marks, one pound of coffee about 30,000 marks; in November the mark traded at 4.2 trillion to the dollar, which had been worth 4.2 marks in July 1914. More than 1700 presses in 133 print-works were running day and night to produce banknotes which would be worthless on the eve of the following day. With prices rising at such an accelerating speed, in the end doubling or trebling several times a day, those who depended on weekly wages or monthly salaries could not possibly make ends meet.

Only when in November 1923 a newly founded *Rentenbank* (mortgage bank) issued certificates of credit based on the collateral of agricultural and industrial debt as a new currency (*Rentenmark*), did inflation come to a halt. But the basis of this regained monetary stability was in fact, besides a balanced budget, a restricted quantity of currency and restored confidence in its soundness within Germany and abroad.

There had, however, been a few winners, mainly industrialists who used the opportunity to pay off large debts and who benefited from the low cost of German goods abroad. And the German government was relieved of its huge war debts at a single stroke. But the mass of the German people suffered severe losses. Those depending on fixed salaries or on their savings were hit the hardest: white-collar workers, civil servants, pensioners, war widows. And even graver than the immediate material impact was the psychological shock, especially for the middle classes. Millions saw themselves not only robbed of their savings but with the potential loss of their social standing they felt humiliated, angry and bitter. For broad segments of the population economic ruin undermined confidence in the Republic; hostility towards the new democracy grew even among those who had at first voted in support of Weimar Germany. From now on, fear of inflation became another trauma affecting the course of German history, guiding decision making in the field of social and economic politics up to the present day.

Unfortunately, it was only a short period of partial recovery and stabilization that set in after the end of inflation. On the one hand, the industrial sector of the economy now entered a period of rapid growth, by 1927 catching up with pre-war production rates so that by 1929 Germany had again become the world's second industrial power behind the USA. Real wages rose, and the standard of living increased dramatically for large sections of the population. But on the other hand, recovery did not extend to the agrarian sector, domestic investment activity never regained pre-war levels and unemployment remained relatively high: in January 1928 nearly two million Germans were without a job. Moreover, the Weimar economy was far from strong even in this period of apparent boom, because it was very much depending on short-term loans from abroad. These reached 12 billion marks in 1929, out of a total of 25 billion in foreign debts.

This is why Germany was hit extremely hard by the outbreak of the world-wide Depression in 1929. American loans were rapidly withdrawn after the Wall Street Crash of October and with this a steep downturn in the German economy set in. Unemployment rose to more than 5.5 million in January 1932 (30 per cent of the whole workforce). And though every European state struggled with the effects of the Depression, in Germany it caused extremely severe repercussions not only for the government but for society as a whole.

The Weimar Republic was particularly prone to suffer from this crisis because of the manifold interdependencies of state and economy. In view of the numerous strikes during the early years of the Republic, it became increasingly common for governments to settle labour disputes by arbitration. In Germany wages were higher than elsewhere in Europe. At the same time, Bismarck's social policy had not just been continued but its scope had even been expanded by introducing compulsory unemployment insurance in 1927 and the eight-hour working day. Thus, at this time of economic crisis, the proportion of public expenditure devoted to welfare costs and social services exploded. The social budget had risen from 337 million marks in 1913 to 4.751 billion on the eve of the Great Depression. When in the wake of the great crash production was almost halved and tax receipts fell, while one-third of the workforce was without jobs, the state was unable to fulfil its obligations. Accordingly, the last democratic coalition government of the Republic fell over the issue of unemployment insurance.

Again, as with inflation, the state (i.e. democracy), obviously being unable to deal with economic disaster and social crisis, was held responsible. Increasingly, voters now supported those parties whose declared aim was to replace democracy by either a radical revolutionary or by some authoritarian political system. Many of those out of work now joined the communists; many from the ranks of the middle classes now threatened by proletarianization supported the conservative Right or even Hitler's NSDAP. 'It was undoubtedly the depression which precipitated the actual collapse of the Weimar democracy and paved the way for the rise of the Nazis to power.'[1]

Yet, though in some ways the Republic seemed to be doomed from the outset, it was by no means on a downhill one-way road towards destruction. There were also some years of respite and recovery so that the period between stabilization of the currency in 1924 and the resignation of the last parliamentary cabinet in March 1930 have even been labelled 'The Golden Twenties' of the Weimar Republic.

THE 'GOLDEN TWENTIES'

The main feature of this period was Germany's return from her earlier post-war diplomatic isolation. This was largely due to the efforts of Gustav Stresemann, the chairman of the right-wing liberal DVP (German People's Party) – a former monarchist who had gradually become deeply committed to the Republic. After a short span in office as Chancellor from August to November 1923 he was foreign secretary in various cabinets until his untimely death in the month of the crash of the New York Stock Market (October 1929).

His overall foreign policy aim was to 'revise' the consequences of the Treaty of Versailles, which still presented a number of outstanding problems, especially those which were tied up with the issue of reparations. The latter problem resulted from the overwhelming distrust which had guided French foreign policy since the end of the war in the face of any German attempts to recover from the consequences of defeat and regain her former position in European politics. This culminated, in January 1923, in the military occupation of the Ruhr, Germany's industrial heartland, by French and Belgian troops in order to take punitive action because Germany was behind in her reparation payments and was therefore declared to be in default of her treaty obligations.

Stresemann saw that the only way out for Germany was to prove that she was making every effort to meet the demands of the Treaty of Versailles. This, he hoped, would substantially improve relations with

France and England and finally lead to effective modification of the reparations provisions. This 'policy of fulfilment', as nationalist opponents called it, in 1924 led to the adoption of the so-called 'Dawes Plan', which provided American loans to aid German economic development and help Germany meet her reparations obligations. At the same time, relations with France improved. In July 1925 French troops started to leave the Ruhr and in October the Locarno Pact was signed, which marked the beginning of Germany's re-entry into the family of nations. Stresemann achieved this goal by Germany guaranteeing her western frontiers as a further recognition of the validity of the Treaty of Versailles. And he was also careful to balance this agreement with the Western powers by maintaining good relations with Soviet Russia while leaving the issue of the eastern frontiers with Poland open. Finally, in 1927, Germany was accepted into the League of Nations.

Together with the improvement of Germany's economic situation and first successes in the field of foreign politics, Weimar culture achieved international renown during those years of the 'Golden Twenties'. For a short period Berlin became Europe's intellectual capital, outshining even the glamour of Paris, due to a burst of creativity in the fields of arts and sciences. Those were the days of Bertolt Brecht's *Threepenny Opera* and the revolutionary architecture of the Bauhaus School led by Walter Gropius; Marlene Dietrich achieved international stardom in *The Blue Angel*; painters such as Paul Klee, Oskar Kokoschka and Max Beckmann were at the height of their creative powers; Thomas Mann's *Magic Mountain* appeared in 1924; and at the Berlin Academy of Art the Austrian composer Arnold Schönberg taught his students the essentials of atonal music. In some fields, especially in the natural sciences and in painting and literature, the roots of present dazzling achievements pointed back to the turn of the century, but now the arts profited not only from the intellectual hothouse atmosphere of Berlin as a new cultural capital, but also from the fact that public expenditure for education and the arts was substantially higher than during the Wilhelminian years.

However, Weimar culture was a complex and even a deeply divided phenomenon and by no means a pillar to sustain the new Republic. There was a left wing – artists and writers like Georg Grosz, Käthe Kollwitz, Kurt Tucholsky, Arnold Döblin and many others – attacking bourgeois capitalist society, and there were right-wing intellectuals like Ernst Jünger and Möller van den Bruck who criticized parliamentary democracy; there were pervasive trends like a deep sense of cultural pessimism, a revolt against rationalism (as in the case of Expressionism) and often sentimentalism rejecting modernity – altogether a variety of voices, all claiming exclusivity for their themes and styles. The glamour of the Golden Years was a tender plant growing during a short span of partial prosperity and stability, and it was uprooted when a general crisis loomed again after 1932. Weimar culture ended abruptly with Hitler and his party coming to power. Promising careers of numerous artists, scientists and intellectuals were destroyed or at least interrupted; others managed to survive or even thrive in exile; in Germany it was a cultural dark age that followed.

THE FINAL FALL OF THE REPUBLIC

As the collapse of the Republic between 1930 and 1933 proved, the outward stability of the 'Golden Twenties' had not led to an inner consolidation, to a general acceptance of the spirit and the principles of democracy. The main reason for this was that the forces of nationalism – the most potent political agent of the age – would not support the governments of Weimar and their policies. Right from the beginning the Republic lacked the integral element of the nation-state, which is that the consciousness and the aspirations of the nation are compatible with the state, its constitution and its policy. Instead, after defeat and the acceptance of the Treaty of Versailles, German nationalists linked the Weimar Republic to the 'stab-in-the-back' myth.

In the army the majority of leading officers claimed that they would support the national interests but not the democratic state. In particular, those who had formed the backbone of the Prussian-German nation-state, the Protestant middle-classes, could not be won over to the Republic. The churches, university professors, students and schoolteachers, many judges and civil servants were essentially conservative, often even right-wing and anti-democratic in sympathy. During times of crisis the hostility of those groups increased while political liberalism in Germany declined accordingly, as is shown by support for the liberal parties (DDP and DVP), which shrank from 20 per cent of the vote in 1919 to a mere 2 per cent in 1932.

Even Stresemann's successes in the field of foreign policy became the subject of passionate bitter debates within Germany, for example when, on the occasion of the Locarno Treaty, conservatives and groups from the extreme Right accused him of having failed to achieve the impossible, since they demanded the return of Alsace-Lorraine to Germany and the annulment of the war guilt clause of the Versailles Treaty.

And it was also highly significant that in the halcyon days of the Republic, after the premature death of Friedrich Ebert in 1925, the democratic parties (SPD, DDP and Centre Party) failed to get their candidate elected for the office of President of the Republic – on a second ballot, he came only second to the 77-year-old right-wing monarchist Paul von Hindenburg. Hindenburg won because he was regarded as a national hero. In 1914 under his command the Russian army invading Eastern Prussia had been decisively beaten at the battle of Tannenberg. Later, when as chief of staff in autumn 1918 he had to acknowledge military defeat, he became one of the chief propagators of the 'stab-in-the-back' myth. And now, in 1925, he was presented by the political Right as a symbol of moral integrity and uprightness, representing the true interests of the German nation. Though a monarchist at heart, he took his oath to the Republic seriously and until the constitutional crisis of 1930 he exercised the functions of his office correctly.

On the one hand, this election of 1925 had a stabilizing effect because during the course of the second half of the 1920s right-wing conservatives like the German National People's Party (DNVP) made their peace with the Republic, and leading conservative politicians held ministerial posts in a number of centre–right coalition governments. But on the other hand, this first popular election of a President (Ebert had been chosen by the National Assembly) clearly showed that the supporters of democracy were in a minority position, even in the most stable and prosperous period of the Weimar Republic. And when in 1930 after the dissolution of the last coalition government, which at the same time was a breakdown of the last consensus among the Republican forces, Hindenburg was placed in a position of supreme arbiter of the nation, he became a willing executioner for those around him who aimed to replace parliamentary democracy by a more authoritarian rule.

The actual collapse of the Weimar Republic occurred in two stages: the first was the destruction of parliamentary government and the second the failure of the Conservatives' attempts to establish a non-parliamentary regime without granting Hitler and his party access to power.

The beginning of the end can be dated back to 27 March 1930, when the coalition government led by the SPD fell over the failure to agree on adequate measures to deal with rising unemployment in the wider context of economic recession. This was taken as a sign of the inability of democracy in general and of democratic parties in particular to lead the nation in times of crisis. Hindenburg appointed as chancellor Heinrich Brüning, a prominent member of the Centre Party with a reputation as a financial expert, who was known to have long-standing reservations about the democratic constitutional system.

Brüning's cabinet lacked majority support in parliament. However, according to the letter of the constitution, in cases where there was no parliamentary majority to back the government, the President could authorize the Chancellor to rule by presidential decree. Provisions set out in the constitution for the exceptional situation of extreme emergency became the rule for governing the country for the next three years. Moreover, Brüning's actual policies also contributed decisively to the ever-growing crisis in parliamentary democracy.

He pursued a course of austere deflationary policies, not so much to meet the economic crisis as to achieve his foreign policy aim: to convince the Allies that Germany simply had no resources to continue reparation payments. To this end taxes were raised, public expenditure was reduced, severe cuts in wages and salaries were introduced and the government even exacerbated the unemployment situation – taken together these were belt-tightening measures at the cost of the well-being of millions of Germans. And the social consequences of this policy were a further rise of political radicalism on the Left as well as on the Right.

This became evident when, after having rejected one of Brüning's finance bills, Hindenburg dissolved parliament and new elections took place in September 1932. This time radical opponents of the Republic achieved spectacular gains. The Communists won 10.6 per cent of the votes, which gave them 77 seats, and Hitler's NSDAP achieved its electoral breakthrough with 18.3 per cent of the total vote (6.4 million). With 107 seats it was now the second largest party, second only to the SPD (143 seats), and thus this election had finally given a clear majority to those parties which were the declared enemies of the Weimar Republic and her present constitution.

The result of this constitutional deadlock was that from now on parliament, the core of any democratic state, was excluded from the political decision-making process. This now lay with a small group of anti-parliamentarian Conservatives who relied on the authority and the charisma of President Hindenburg. At the same time, violence was back again on the streets of many major German cities. In Berlin, in particular, competing rival gangs, the paramilitary organizations of the Communists and the SA (the Stormtroopers of the Nazis), clashed in bloody skirmishes, all this against the background of growing social misery.

The paradoxical conclusion of the 1930 elections for Brüning and the Conservatives, as well as for the SPD, was not to risk any further elections in order to stop a further growth of the radical parties, especially the NSDAP. Therefore, the SPD chose to tolerate the Brüning government. And when in 1932 Hindenburg's term of office came to an end, in order to stop Hitler the moderate parties (including the SPD) now supported Hindenburg, who was re-elected after a bitter campaign. Soon afterwards Brüning fell victim to the constitutional constellation he had helped to create. Dependent only on the support of the President, he was dismissed when Hindenburg was persuaded by his closest advisers that even Brüning, who in a desperate last attempt had ordered the dissolution of the Nazi Stormtroopers and the Communist Red Front Fighters, had still been too accommodating to the forces of democracy.

Between 30 May 1932, the day when Brüning resigned, and 30 January 1933, the day when Hitler was appointed Chancellor, the final catastrophe of the Weimar Republic unfolded. It was brought about by intrigues and backstairs machinations with von Papen and Schleicher – who both followed Brüning in the office of Chancellor – as protagonists and it was hastened by the results of two further parliamentary elections on 31 July and 6 November 1932. The first gave Hitler's party its best ever result in a free election: 37.8 per cent of the vote and 230 out of 608 seats, which made the NSDAP the largest party in the *Reichstag* for the first time. And though they lost 34 seats in the second election of that year, after Chancellor von Papen had parliament dissolved because of a spectacular vote of no confidence, deadlock was not resolved. Now Papen and others, like Alfred Hugenberg, the influential chairman of the German National People's Party (DNVP), came round to the view that the NSDAP must become part of a conservative–nationalist coalition government. So in the end, believing they would be able to control him by conferring an official position upon him, a reluctant Hindenburg was persuaded to appoint Hitler German Chancellor on 30 January 1933. The fate of the Weimar Republic was sealed because Hitler was resolved not to be just another chancellor in the long chain of Weimar's chancellors but to turn Germany into Hitler's Germany.

It might not have been doomed by the troubled circumstances of its beginnings, but obviously the fragile Weimar democracy never got the chance to consolidate to such an extent that it could withstand the numerous strains and stresses caused by the almost continuous crisis which was the essence of its short history. At the same time no single factor alone is sufficient to explain its dissolution. There were unfavourable surroundings as well as structural weaknesses (e.g. Versailles and the Weimar Constitution); failures on the part of its supporters (the SPD at times more or less abdicating its responsibility); and hostile assaults from its opponents. But above all, it was the growing disaffection of the German middle classes which brought the Republic down. It was not a democracy without democrats, but a democracy with too few democrats. And though it might seem that the final events before Hitler's appointment were more in the nature of avoidable accidents, in fact, parliamentary democracy had already collapsed when the last coalition government resigned in 1930, and dedicated reactionaries within Germany's political and military elites began to look for authoritarian alternatives to democracy. Hitler did not destroy the Republic: the fortress he took was already in ruins.

9

Hitler's Germany

HITLER'S BEGINNINGS

Never, before Hitler came to power, had a single individual – not even Bismarck – shaped the course of German history so decisively that within a dozen years the country first threatened to dominate the whole of Europe and shortly afterwards was on the brink of total extinction. At the same time his short reign of crime and terror marked the climax of the horrors of the twentieth century.

Adolf Hitler, an Austrian, born in 1889 near the Bavarian border, came from a petty bourgeois family. Orphaned as a teenager, he did poorly at school, went to Vienna at the age of 19, applied in vain to the painting school of the Academy of Fine Arts and to the School of Architecture. He eked out a scanty living as a part-time decorator and postcard artist, spending his nights in hostels for homeless men and passing his days walking aimlessly around the old imperial city or reading extensively, though without plan. And here, amidst the mixed population of the impoverished districts of Vienna, the introverted, resentful and lonely young man formed those prejudices and hatreds which became the stuff of his basic political doctrines: his crude Darwinian conviction of the survival of the fittest together with his admiration of naked power, his fanatical nationalism combined with a theory of a Germanic master race destined to rule the world, his profound hatred of Jews and of democracy and liberalism.

In 1913 Hitler left Austria and went to Munich, where he welcomed the outbreak of the First World War as a relief from his personal misery. He volunteered for the army and served with distinction on the Western Front. When the war ended he was in a military hospital, consumed with violent hatred for the 'November criminals' and, according to his book *Mein Kampf* (My Struggle), it was then that he decided 'to become a politician'. In 1919 he joined a tiny Munich right-wing group, the *Deutsche Arbeiterpartei* (German Workers' Party), and having discovered his extraordinary talent for oratory and demagoguery became its leading speaker. In 1920 the party was renamed *National-Sozialistische Deutsche Arbeiterpartei* (NSDAP, National Socialist German Workers' Party) and in July 1921 Hitler became its leader.

Though he managed to propel himself to the forefront of Munich's right-wing political scene, Hitler was still merely a figure of local renown when in 1923, at the climax of the first great crisis of the Weimar Republic, he waged his first bid for power. But his putsch of 9 November, a large demonstration through the streets of Munich modelled on the Italian fascists' March on Rome, yet hastily and badly organized, was a dismal failure, though in the event it would give Hitler considerable national publicity in the ensuing trial (in which he was sentenced to only a short prison term).

Hitler thereupon switched tactics and decided from now on to seek power only by constitutional means – at the same time, however, always emphasizing the anti-parliamentary nature of his aims and his party. And for Hitler changing his strategy merely meant looking for an alternative path to power in order to implement his political programme, which was never to be altered throughout the whole of his political career.

HITLER'S MESSAGE

He had used his time in the relatively comfortable circumstances of Landsberg prison to put down and demonstrate at length his fundamental political aims in his rambling memoirs *Mein Kampf*. These culminated in the final dictum: 'Germany will either be a world power or there will be no Germany.'[1] This was the core of Hitler's crude racial theory which assigned to the 'Ayrian' race, embodied above all by the Germans, a pre-eminent role in history, which he considered as a struggle of survival between the human races. To this end the Germans would need ample *Lebensraum* (living space) – i.e. land and soil – mainly in the east, which was to be won by conquering and subjugating Russia. Having accomplished this, the new Third Reich of the Germans was to stand a thousand years. Hitler regarded the Jews as the most dangerous counterpart in this epochal struggle and in this context he proclaimed Bolshevism, alongside 'British imperialism' and 'American plutocracy' to be 'a product of Jewish thought'.[2]

Though the fundamentals of Hitler's political ideology would form the guidelines of his later politics of war and extermination, his programme did not provide the key to his spectacular success story. This was connected with his outstanding organizational and propaganda skills and, finally, with the immense energy he derived from his conviction that he had been endowed by fate with the power to lead Germany out of despair and humiliation to glory and greatness. And this went together with an overwhelming feeling of hatred and revenge, which was repeatedly given free rein in his speeches: hatred against those who had ridiculed and derided him and against everybody and everything that stood in the way of his and Germany's road to power. Such emotional intensity, coupled with his natural rhetorical skill and the deliberate employment of the means and tricks of demagoguery, led to pseudo-hypnotic performances which induced mass hysteria among his audiences.

Usually, long before Hitler entered the assembly hall, masses of swastika flags, martial music and long lines of uniformed Stormtroopers put people in the right mood. Then the 'Führer' made his appearance. After having reminded his audience of the humiliating defeat of 1918 he accused the 'November criminals' – Marxists and Jews and those parties who had assented to the shameful Treaty of Versailles – aroused the hatred of the crowd against the 'system of Weimar', made it join his own blazing fury and his cry for revenge until, in the end, they were eager to follow him as their *Führer* who would guide them on the road towards salvation. To this end, he proclaimed, he would lead the Germans on the third way, which was neither the way of capitalism nor that of socialism but the way of nationalism, where class divisions were made irrelevant by the *Volksgemeinschaft*, the national community uniting leaders and followers irrespective of their social background. And to this end his party, the NSDAP, presented itself as a party of national integration rather than a class-bound interest group.

The message of Hitler's speeches was reinforced by demonstrations and rallies of the party, and especially by his readiness to use violence against his political enemies. Engaging his Stormtroopers in street fighting against the communists was also a means of demonstrating his resolution for direct action and thus to stress the difference between the parliamentary democratic parties and the Nazi 'movement', which was paramilitary in organization and violent in action.

Yet neither his message, with its many appeals to the fears and prejudices of his German contemporaries, nor the skilful way it was presented and spread, gave Hitler sufficient success at the polls to seize power by constitutional means. At the election of 1928, at the height of the 'Golden Years' of Weimar, he received a meagre 2.6 per cent of the popular vote. It required the bitter years of the Depression, together with all those secondary effects of the economic disaster, to transform the National Socialists from a fringe group to a major political force. But even later, as long as there were free elections Hitler never won an absolute majority of the votes. Still, being the leader of the strongest party gave him sufficient backing to become a major figure in the end game for power.

HITLER'S SUPPORTERS

Who were the people that voted for Hitler? Even before 1933 the party was drawing on a broad social spectrum of support. Neither party membership nor the votes it gained were restricted to the petty bourgeoisie – as a class highly threatened in its social status by recent developments. Though the party's most stable vote came from Protestant members of the middle and lower-middle classes who felt endangered by the effects of industrial modernization, they were joined by representatives of the professional and commercial elites. Membership records show that businessmen, Protestant pastors, senior civil servants and the professions in general were overrepresented before 1933.

As far as big business was concerned, though on the whole it was decidedly critical of the social and labour-relations policies of the Weimar Republic and despite Hitler's overtures to these circles after 1927, only a few industrialists like the steel magnate Fritz Thyssen gave direct financial support to the NSDAP. Support from workers was by no means marginal, yet before 1933 restricted mainly to those who had no links either to the trade unions or the socialist parties, so that by 1933 not more than a third of the party's membership came from the working class, although workers as a whole formed about half of the electorate.

Apart from social distinctions it was in the first place the younger generation which was attracted by the NSDAP:

1930 36.8 per cent of the members and 26.2 per cent of its leadership were 30 years of age or younger. No less than 43 per cent of those joining the party between 1930 and 1933 were between 18 and 30 and 27 per cent between 30 and 40 years of age. ... In comparison to the SPD and even more so to the parties representing the middle classes the NSDAP was the party of the young generation. ... In the *Reichstag* elected on 14 September 1930 only 10 per cent of the SPD-members were under 40, whereas it were 60 per cent with the parliamentary party of the NSDAP, as well as with the KPD.[3]

This is a clear indication of the fact that young people preferred what they regarded as revolutionary movements to the traditional political parties and a further indication of the unpopularity of the new democracy with the new generation. And that is why many turned to Hitler, who promised them a new Germany in which all the present difficulties would be solved under the undisputed leadership of the *Führer*.

At the same time the messages Hitler offered – clad in catchy slogans – as well as the often violent action of his myrmidons appealed to all those who felt lost or insecure in times of rapid change and thorough modernization. When he strongly criticized and attacked the increasing market share of department stores, or when he conjured up the image of the sturdy peasant who cultivates his soil and defends his hearth and home with his own hands as the model of the Germanic race, instead of being convinced by arguments people were overwhelmed by sentiments. Paradoxically, while offering protection against a modern world of change, competition and conflict, the regime at the same time made efficient use of the latest achievements of modern technology: Goebbels had his message propagated by the radio and not by the town crier of medieval times and until the end Hitler set high hopes on the development of new 'wonder-weapons' of mass destruction.

HITLER'S SEIZURE OF POWER

When Hitler was appointed Chancellor on 30 January 1933 he still had not actually 'seized power', as the official myth would soon suggest. But he set out immediately, with utmost determination, speed and ruthlessness to gather all the reins of government and administration in his own hands and to consolidate his hold over the German people. As he was still resolved to achieve all this by pseudo-legal means, parliament was dissolved, and in search of a parliamentary majority, new elections were set for 5 March. Yet, in spite of massive propaganda and severe limitations for the parties of the Left, together with the first acts of terror, Hitler's NSDAP with 43.9 per cent of the vote again failed to gain an overall majority (Social Democrats 18.3 per cent, Communists 12.3 per cent, Catholic centre 11.2 per cent, Conservatives 8 per cent; – the Liberals were marginalized to a mere 1.8 per cent). But this did not prevent Hitler from destroying parliamentary democracy, abolishing the rule of law and uprooting venerable German political traditions.

Here he could take advantage of a fortuitous incident. On 28 February the *Reichstag* building was set on fire and Hitler exploited the opportunity to blame the Communists and made Hindenburg issue a 'Presidential Decree for the Protection of the People and the State', which virtually abrogated all civil liberties, as they were set down in the Weimar Constitution, 'until further notice'. This was followed by the so-called 'Enabling Law' of 23 March, which 'legalized' the destruction of democracy since it gave the government power to rule by decree for the next four years, and which, in fact, was repeatedly extended and remained valid until 1945. From now on arbitrary acts, which did not even need the signature of the President, could replace parliamentary legislation. This overthrow of the remnants of democracy was achieved by constitutional means because Hitler got the two-thirds majority of the votes needed for amending the constitution. After the Communist members of the *Reichstag* and 21 of the Social Democrats had been prevented from attending the meeting, all parties with the exception of the SDP, voted for a law which legalized the foundation of Hitler's dictatorship.

The destruction of democracy was naturally followed by the abolition of the party system. In July 1933 all parties became illegal except the NSDAP, which was declared the only true national party.

Democracy, parliamentary government and the constitutional guarantee of human rights had been relatively recent achievements in the course of German history. But when on the first anniversary of 30 January 1933 German federalism was destroyed by abolishing the parliaments of the *Länder* and turning their governments into subunits of the central administration, a venerable tradition of German political life, which reached back to the Middle Ages, was violated. Even under

Bismarck Germany had been a federal union; now, for the first time in history, it had become a centralized state. Dictatorship was complete when Hindenburg died on 2 August 1934 and Hitler merged the offices of Chancellor and President, styled himself *Führer und Reichskanzler* and took command of the army; from now on soldiers as well as judges and civil servants had to swear personal oaths of obedience to Hitler, who now united the essence of all forms of authority in his person.

In his seizure of power Hitler had been aided by the conservative elites who had not only brought him into office but were also essential for the effective use of that power. Even after their political leaders like Franz von Papen or Hugenberg began to realize that Hitler was not to be manipulated for their own ends, the fateful coalition between the two forces survived for a while and helped Hitler to consolidate his dictatorship. In the end, these old elites became the main tools of the new regime, which made use of the efficiency of the established administration, the productivity of German industry, the fighting power of the German army and especially the expertise of its military leaders.

At the same time the traditional institutions of the state were either abolished or occupied and perverted by the NSDAP. Soon there were no longer any cabinet meetings and political decision making became more and more a matter of gaining direct access to the *Führer*, whose will alone could not only override existing law but was in itself the law. In fact, this new Germany was a state without a constitution because Hitler knew that absolute personal power is only possible when chaos reigns – so that when disputes arose between competing political and administrative agencies it would be left to him, the dictator, to deliver the ultimate decision.

And chaos reigned indeed. On the one side there still existed the state administration and the judiciary and on the other side there was the Party with its own continually expanding network of organizations and institutions, which with its block wardens eventually reached into every household. And the paramilitary forces of the NSDAP, first the SA (*Sturm-Abteilung*) and later the SS (*Schutzstaffel*), which had originally been Hitler's special protection squad, soon took over essential police functions, as, for example, in the field of state security. They were able to arrest, detain, imprison, torture and even murder regardless of the law and established rules of juridical procedure. And soon as well as ordinary prisons there were the first concentration camps, originally installed by the SA for political opponents of the regime.

These Stormtroopers, with a membership of about 400,000 at the end of 1932, had played an important role in Hitler's rise to power and under their ambitious leader Ernst Röhm now propagated unwelcome notions of the need for a 'second revolution'. At the same time they aspired to take over the role of the army and thereby threatened the still unstable alliance between Hitler and the generals. In this situation Hitler was persuaded by Röhm's rivals to order a purge – on 30 June 1934 the leaders of the SA, along with other political opponents, were murdered by SS units on the unproven accusation that they had been planning a plot. Though an open act of violence, many Germans were relieved that the dangerous elements had obviously been put in their place and from now on Hitler's alliance with the army was strengthened.

On the whole, there was not much opposition to crush and though the instruments of terror and suppression had been prepared, they never needed to be extensively employed in order to deal with a revolt or even a popular uprising. After the Communists had been brutally suppressed, there was hardly any resistance when the other parties were dissolved. Those who stuck to their convictions either emigrated, like the leading SPD members, or withdrew from public life and out of fear of arrest led a double life of outward conformity while withholding their real views. Others tried to make their peace with the new regime. Although up to 1933 the NSDAP had not gained much support from the Catholics, the Centre Party had assented to the 'Enabling Law'. In return for Hitler's promise of concessions concerning a free exercise of their faith a concordat between Germany and the Church of Rome seemed to seal a tacit approval of Hitler's dictatorship, until, later on, the open struggle would be resumed – because, in fact, there was no common ground for the Christian creed and Hitler's *Weltanschauung*.

But, on the whole, most Germans saw no reason for opposing the new regime. And though correct estimates are difficult to make, after only five years an overwhelming majority of the German people had been won over by Hitler. They might not join the NSDAP but they believed in or even adored the *Führer*, dazzled by his successes and achievements.

And they were not even greatly irritated by occasional acts of open violence or rumours about the brutal acts of terror done behind the scenes by the SS or the *Gestapo*, the secret police. As long as 'others' were the victims – communists and socialists, open critics of the regime and ethnic minorities like the Jews – people might shrug their shoulders and accept such measures as being necessary to establish 'law and order'. And when there was reason for anger or criticism, provoked by acts of the administration or party officials, people would mutter: 'If only the *Führer* knew.'

HITLER'S 'ACHIEVEMENTS'

Far more important than skilful propaganda or the thinly veiled threat of terror were the achievements of Hitler's policy, which not only allowed the Germans to tolerate the new regime but gave it broad genuinely popular support. First of all, there was a kind of economic miracle which gave new hope of stability and prosperity after so many years of economic disaster. An obvious sign of economic recovery was a sharp decline in the unemployment rate, which was reduced from 29.9 per cent in 1932 to a mere 1.9 per cent in 1938, when even Great Britain and the USA had to struggle with 12.9 per cent and 26.4 per cent of the workforce without jobs.

Aided by a general upswing in the world economy the new administration made a U-turn and replaced Brüning's policies of monetary and budgetary restraint by expansionist policies of massive job creation even at the price of growing public debt. Government-sponsored public work programmes were launched, among them projects for the construction of the famous *Autobahnen* (super highways). When Hitler based Germany's economic policy on deficit financing, he was not guided by any economic theories and he did not aim just at regaining general prosperity without inflation for the mass of the German people. Instead, his overriding interest lay in the preparation for the conquest of *Lebensraum*, of expanded living space for the Germanic race in Central and Eastern Europe. Therefore, from the very beginning rearmament was the ultimate goal of the new German economic policies, as was clearly demonstrated by a Four-Year Plan developed in 1936. The huge loans needed to pay for the preparation of the future war remained unredeemed and were to be paid back by the conquered enemy after Hitler's final victory: 'ultimate economic salvation was predicated on a successful war of conquest'.[4]

However, as the great majority of the people were ignorant of the true aims and the fundamental problems of the regime's new economic policies, confidence and faith in a brighter future prevailed. And, indeed, most sections of the population seemed to be better off than during the final months of the Republic. Though, in fact, they had lost the protection of the closely knit network of social legislation they had enjoyed during the 'Golden Years' of Weimar, as well as their right of collective bargaining and protection from arbitrary dismissal (in May 1933 the trade unions were wound up and supplanted by the NS-dominated German Labour Front), yet most workers appreciated the fact that they once more had employment. Moreover, many were impressed by the fact that the regime seemed concerned about the well-being of the workers: for example, the new recreation society *Kraft durch Freude* (Strength through Joy) offered organized holidays – even to foreign countries.

Industrialists were, of course, the beneficiaries of the suppression of the unions and heavy industry and armaments manufacture prospered as the result of a policy that ran under the motto:'preparing for war in times of peace'. And though this goal in general and the Four Years' Plan in particular implied severe limitations for economic freedom through state control, the capitalistic structure of the German economy remained basically unchanged.

Farmers were also undoubtedly better off than before, or at least able to hold on to their land, even though the production and the pricing of foodstuffs came under strict controls. And when official doctrine proclaimed the importance and glory of 'blood and soil', many were convinced of a brighter future for the *Reichsnährstand* (the class which provides food for the Reich), as the peasants were now officially called.

And the professionals, lawyers and judges, teachers and professors, doctors and higher civil servants benefited from the dismissal of political opponents from the civil service and from the growing persecutions of the Jews.

Paradoxically, those who had formed the backbone of the NSDAP, the commercial sector of the German middle class, did not profit from the new economic and social policies. Although Hitler's propaganda had promised them the suppression of the big department stores, the government continued to give preference to large-scale business.

Yet, all things considered, the economic policies of the government were a key factor in Hitler's early and genuine general popularity, which was needed to prepare the Germans to follow him on his way towards the realization of his 'Grand Design': the establishment of a German world power as an empire founded on the basis of the superiority of the Germanic race.

THE TOOLS OF TOTALITARIANISM

However, to attain this goal more was needed than general content-
ment with regained stability and the prospect of future prosperity: to
gain victory in a second great war and to establish the dominion of the
Germanic race over a new vast empire, the Germans had to be
educated and drilled in order to turn them into obedient retainers of
their *Führer*. To this end an array of mass organizations encompassed
and watched over every aspect of the lives of individuals.

In the first place, there was the Party, the NSDAP, which, according
to Hitler's will, was 'to weld the German people into a solid nation',
and its numerous affiliates for every age and every occupation, including, among many others, the NSKK (National Socialist Motor
Transport Corps) for car owners, charities like the Winter Aid or
women's organizations like the NS *Frauenschaft*. And great attention
was, of course, paid to winning over and organizing the young generation. From the age of ten onwards children were expected to join first
the *Deutsche Jungvolk* and then the *Hitlerjugend* (for boys) or the
Jungmädel and then the *Bund Deutscher Mädel* (League of German
Maidens) for girls. Here the basis for a new kind of society was to be
laid, an organic, harmonious community without class antagonisms,
held together by the bond of a common Nordic race and a common
political faith. And at the same time paramilitary activities and attitudes were to prepare future soldiers for the war to come.

Growing support for Hitler's regime was also due to massive propaganda on the radio, in the newspapers and at spectacular party rallies.
And Hitler's minister of propaganda, Joseph Goebbels, paid particular
attention to the management of cultural life, which was to be purged
of 'Jewish decadence'. To this end, Goebbels, by comprehensive and
strict censorship, made sure that nothing was published or exhibited
that was not approved of by his ministry. On 10 May 1933, the books
of 'un-German' authors – among them Heinrich and Thomas Mann
and Bertold Brecht – were burnt in a public bonfire on Berlin's central
thoroughfare *Unter den Linden*. From now on, only 'race-conscious'
'German art' was to take the place of 'Degenerate Art'. In the years
between 1933 and 1938 German intellectual life was impoverished by
a purge of all forms of modernism, which drove many, among them the
very best authors, artists and scientists, into exile.

Taken all together, it was a mixture of terror and propaganda, of
violence and seduction which achieved what was called

Gleichschaltung, i.e. the co-ordination and bringing into line of the Germans in order to turn them into instruments of their *Führer*. And, above all, it was a new appeal to emotions that accounted for much of the attraction Hitler and his Party had for a great many Germans, especially among the younger generation. The politics of Weimar had often meant tedious discussions, rational arguments weighing all sides of a question. Now there was only one message and it was about Germany as a united and homogeneous community that was on her way back to glory and greatness, on her way to a future which was linked to a great past, to the age of Frederick the Great and the German emperors of medieval times. And this message was not argued but rather presented again and again by symbolic acts, such as Hitler meeting Hindenburg in the Garrison Church of Potsdam on 21 March 1933, by impressive spectacles like the yearly, skilfully arranged party rallies at Nuremberg, or by the Berlin Olympic Games in 1936.

FOREIGN POLICY ON THE ROAD TO WAR

In the course of a few years Hitler had succeeded in restoring national pride for the great majority of the German people. This was mainly the result of his victories on the foreign policy front. Here the object of all the Weimar governments had always been the revision of the terms of the Treaty of Versailles. Stresemann and others had attempted to achieve this through bilateral or multilateral negotiations and agreements with Germany's former enemies. These efforts had culminated in the Treaty of Locarno and Germany's membership of the League of Nations.

But after Stresemann's death there was a new tone in German foreign policy until Hitler finally unleashed a policy of confrontation and even bullying: his first foreign policy coup was to have Germany withdrawn from the League of Nations in October 1933. And although the annulment of the Treaty of Versailles also stood high on Hitler's agenda, right from the very beginning he aspired to more than that. What he intended was to pursue an aggressive and expansionist foreign policy: to conquer new *Lebensraum* in the east and secure these lands through 'relentless Germanization', as he disclosed to high-ranking officers of the army as early as 3 February 1933.

But, first, he succeeded in reaching territorial and political revisions of the Treaty of Versailles by peaceful means, revisions that would leave Germany in a better position to wage another war. Within the short span of only three years, between 1935 and 1938, Hitler gained a whole series of impressive victories, which dazzled the Germans. In January 1935 the Saarland on the western border was returned to Germany. France had enjoyed the fruits of the coal production of this area, according to the terms of the Versailles settlement; now a plebiscite was held, with the result that a majority of 91 per cent voted for 'coming home into the *Reich*'.

Hitler's next successful stroke was a blatant violation of the terms of Versailles, when he introduced universal military conscription in March 1934. And though this step was censured by Britain, France and Italy as well as by the League of Nations, only three months later Britain signalled her acceptance of German rearmament by concluding a naval treaty with Berlin, intended to forestall another naval arms race. Then, in March 1936, Hitler sent troops into the demilitarized zone on the left bank of the Rhine, again in clear defiance of the Peace Treaty, again occasioning only limited protests from abroad.

After having restored full German sovereignty, he embarked on his programme of territorial expansion. In March 1938, following the exertion of considerable pressure on the Austrian government, Austria was annexed when German troops crossed the border and were met by near-universal acclaim of the Austrian people. With this coup Hitler had created the Greater German *Reich* which had been on the political agenda as far back as the times of the 1848 German Revolution, and with this political triumph he had obviously surpassed even Bismarck's achievement, for again there was only muted international reaction.

Such a policy of 'appeasement' – by means of which the Western powers, especially Britain, wanted to buy further time for their own rearmament and at the same time sought to accommodate Germany's 'legitimate' desires for regaining an adequate position in the international concert of the Great Powers – reached its climax when Hitler, only a few months after the annexation of Austria, turned his attention to his next victim, Czechoslovakia. Here, the radical *Sudeten* German Party had managed to create unrest among the approximately 3 million-strong German ethnic group in the northern border regions, providing Berlin with a pretext to prepare for military invasion. On the brink of war, very much contrary to Hitler's true intentions, military action was averted by British diplomacy. At an international summit conference in Munich in October 1938, Czechoslovakia – which was neither represented nor even consulted – was forced to cede her northern and western border territories to Germany. At the same time the four powers – Germany, France, Italy and Great Britain – guaranteed the integrity of what remained of Czechoslovakia, with the result that, as soon as March 1939, the German army invaded Prague, and Bohemia and Moravia were transformed into a German protectorate.

Next, Hitler turned his attention to Poland. In May 1939 he informed the High Command of the Army of his intention to conquer Poland. Given the record of the policies of appeasement he was convinced that he could easily ignore the fact that Poland's independence had only recently been guaranteed by Britain. Besides, Germany's diplomatic position improved spectacularly when in August 1939, in a surprise move, Hitler concluded a non-aggression pact with Stalin, which not only relieved him of the risk of a two-front war, but also (in a secret section) arranged the details for a fourth partition of Poland and the Baltic States between Germany and the Soviet Union. On the pretext of a border incident staged by the Germans, in the early hours of 1 September 1939 Hitler's army invaded Poland without a declaration of war.

However, this time Britain and France stood firm, which meant that with this new act of aggression Hitler had, in fact, unleashed the Second World War. During the next two years he would crown the succession of diplomatic achievements with a series of stunning military victories. Introducing the strategy of the *Blitzkrieg* (lightning-fast war), which combined attacks from the air, massed tank assaults, and swiftly moving infantry, Poland was defeated and dismembered after only four weeks. Her western territories were annexed by the *Reich*, the eastern parts and the Baltic States by the Soviet Union and the rest became the 'General Government' under German occupation.

In June 1940, after several months of a 'phoney war' of nearly total inaction in the west, and following a brilliant campaign of only six weeks, France suffered a humiliating defeat, and was forced to sign an armistice that divided the country into a northern zone, occupied by the Germans, and a southern zone, eventually governed by a collaborationist regime. Earlier on, Denmark and Norway had been occupied in order to secure Scandinavia against the British, and Luxemburg, Belgium and Holland had suffered the same fate when German forces invaded France from the north.

In the summer of 1940 Hitler was at the very height of his power. Within a few months, striding from victory to victory, he had led

Germany to mastery over the European continent west of the Russian border. And though this time Germans had not greeted the beginning of the war with enthusiam and had taken up arms in a sombre mood, most of them now unreservedly applauded his success. Had Hitler died in 1940, he might have been remembered as one of the greatest German political leaders of all time by those who were neither willing nor able to take a closer look at the aims and methods of his policies. For behind the dazzling façade of rapid military triumphs there lurked the dark abyss of genocide and extermination, as well as the first forebodings of ultimate defeat for Hitler's Germany.

Up to now, Hitler's victories had been easy victories; neither in his attacks on the Weimar Republic nor in the field of foreign policy had he ever been forced to deal with determined and resourceful resistance. The way from democracy to dictatorship had already been paved by his conservative allies who had also achieved the termination of Germany's obligaton for reparations in 1932; the 'system of Versailles' was already crumbling when Hitler started his series of violations of the Treaty, and cracks were showing in the relations between the Western Allies of the First World War. When the war was finally unleashed, the brave Polish army was never a match for the German forces, which had the advantage of the latest technical improvements in armaments. And on the western front, the French army of 1940, inadequately equipped and without the slightest desire for war, could in no way be compared to that of 1914.

Even more importantly, although Hitler had always aimed at war, the war he got did not exactly correspond to the global constellation he had always hoped for. Originally his plan for the foundation of a German super-power in Central and Eastern Europe had rested on the idea of a German–British partnership. He had always admired the way Britain had ruled her world-wide Empire and he regarded a British–German alliance as the only means for Europe to meet the danger of the rapidly rising power of the USA in the West and the USSR in the East. To this end, he had envisaged a global division of power with Germany dominating the European continent and Britain being free to rule her maritime and colonial empire. This is why he had repeatedly wooed the British by means of an often rather crude diplomacy, and even after the outbreak of the war and the defeat of Britain's ally France he still hoped finally to win London as a partner.

However, when Winston Churchill replaced Neville Chamberlain as prime minister in May 1940, it became obvious that Great Britain

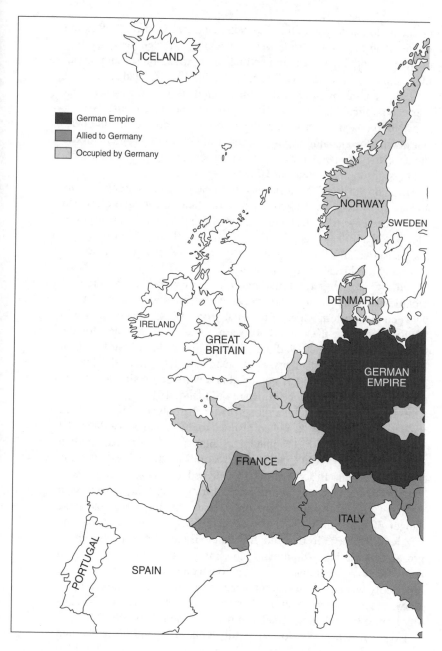

Map 8 The German domination of Europe, December 1941 (adapted from *Das* frontispiece).

Deutsche Reich und der Zweite Weltkrieg, vol. 5 (Stuttgart, 1988),

was more determined than ever to keep on fighting. Here, for the first time, Hitler met with firm resistance. By September 1940 it had become clear that an invasion of England was not practicable. Instead, Hitler now returned to his original ambition: the conquest of Eastern Europe. On 22 June 1941 the German army invaded Russian territory. Earlier on, German troops had already attacked and occupied Yugoslavia and Greece and had come to the assistance of Italy in North Africa, where the German Africa Corps under General Rommel drove the British back into Egypt. War was definitely proliferating and when Japan, Hitler's other main ally, attacked the American fleet at Pearl Harbor on 7 December 1941, Hitler used this opportunity to declare war on the USA. Thus the European War was finally turned into the Second World War.

TOTAL WAR, GENOCIDE AND DEFEAT

In the East Hitler had hoped for another *Blitzkrieg*. However, after dazzling initial victories, by the end of the year the war had become what Hitler had always sought to avoid, a war of attrition. And the huge expansion of the military area was soon to reveal that the German military capacity was in fact strained to the point of exhaustion. Even before the Battle of Stalingrad marked the final turning point, there was no longer a realistic chance of Germany winning the war.

From its very beginning the war in the East did not comply with the rules of 'civilized warfare' as laid down by international law, but was conceived by Hitler, by the SS and also soon by some of his generals as a 'racial war', aimed at the total annihilation of the enemy. As a war for the conquest of *Lebensraum*, of new soil for German settlements, it was understood to justify not only the future expulsion of much of the Slavic population of Russia from the lands west of the Ural Mountains, but also the physical elimination of sections of the native elite. Thus the infamous 'commissar order' authorized all units of the German army to execute captured Bolshevik leaders and Red Army commissars, instead of treating them as prisoners of war – unbridled barbarism was finally unleashed.

At the same time this war of extinction culminated in what Hitler and his executioners called 'the Final Solution of the Jewish question': the systematic murder of millions of Jewish men, women and children, which has come to be labelled 'Holocaust', though this is 'essentially a misnomer'[5] (originally it referred to a sacrificial burnt offering whereas, in fact, Hitler's policy of genocide was nothing but an enormous, singularly heinous, crime). And this was not a by-product of the war, but an essential part of Hitler's racial policy, which was even more rigorously enforced at a time when military defeat became more or less a certainty.

The monstrous, factory-like slaughter in the extermination camps, which began on a large scale in spring 1942, was the climax of a policy of discrimination and persecution, which had started as soon as Hitler seized power. On 1 April 1933 a boycott of all Jewish businesses was proclaimed and soon Jewish civil servants such as judges and professors were dismissed. Then the Nuremberg Laws (1935) turned Jews into second-class citizens who, among other discriminations, were no longer allowed to marry Germans. In 1938 the campaign against Jews entered a stage of open violence when on 9 November, in the course of a 'spontaneous' pogrom, Stormtroopers and other Party radicals burnt synagogues, attacked Jews, looted Jewish property and even murdered 91 people of Jewish descent. From now on German Jews had become a stigmatized, oppressed community in their own homeland. Many thousands were arrested and sent to concentration camps and whoever had the opportunity and the means tried to emigrate.

After the beginning of the war, this policy of exclusion and oppression was followed by a second phase of NS 'Jewish policy', when plans for a 'territorial solution' were discussed: i.e. to force all European Jews to settle either on the island of Madagascar or in Eastern Siberia. Yet at the same time plans were developed for the 'final solution' in the form of physical mass extermination and from spring 1942 onwards were put into practice in special camps on Polish soil (such as Auschwitz, Treblinka etc.). In the course of the following three years six million Jews were brutally murdered, mostly in the gas chambers, or shot or starved to death. Some four million came from Poland and Russia. But the Jewish communities of every country occupied by Germany were decimated; roughly half of the 500,000 Jews living in Germany and Austria before 1933 were killed.

Never before in the course of European history had such a systematic premeditated mass murder been performed and therefore Auschwitz – and what it stands for – has since 1945 become the latest and most persistent trauma to haunt the Germans and to overshadow their history. Yet unlike before – as with the Thirty Years' War, or Versailles or inflation – Germans could not claim to have been victimized because this time Germans had done the deed, had been the perpetrators. And therefore, right up to the present day, numerous questions have been asked with numerous answers still being discussed, the most basic and important being: How could it happen? Whose responsibility was it? How many were involved? Why was there no protest by the German people?

At the root of it there was anti-Semitism in the sense of a fundamental 'hatred of Jews', which had been endemic throughout European history. It sprang from the Jewish origins of Christianity, because just as for the Jews Christ had been a false Messiah, so for the Christians (in popular legend as well as sometimes even in official theology) the Jews were Christ's own people who had become his killers. And when the Jewish diaspora began to spread far and wide, there were Jewish quarters in many European cities – later called ghettos – where Jews lived according to their own religious laws as separate communities and often became easy targets for those who needed a scapegoat to blame for all sorts of ills in times of general crisis. For throughout the centuries the resentments of a society suffering, for example, from waves of famine or plague or just from the consequences of overpopulation, could easily be turned against such alien minorities. Thus in 1096 the first in a series of major pogroms took place when Christian Crusaders on their way to Palestine killed up to 8000 Jews on their way through the Rhineland. Others were to follow, up to the greatest catastrophe of European Jewry before the twentieth century: the expulsion of more than 100,000 Jews from Spain in 1492.

In Germany Jews also repeatedly suffered from persecution and expulsion in many cities and principalities and here, as elsewhere in Europe, they were reduced to the status of outcasts in a Christian society, who were not allowed to own real property or work as farmers, artisans or merchants, but had to make their living as pedlars, pawnbrokers or money lenders – with the exception of a few families that had managed to rise in the service of some prince and had amassed great fortunes as bankers or brokers.

But with the dissolution of feudalism and the gradual formation of a modern society that rested on the dynamics of economic progress and social change, and under the influence of the tenets of the Enlightenment, the way for the emancipation of the Jews was opened and between 1780 and 1870 they gradually achieved the status of citizens, which gave them equality in rights and sometimes even equal opportunities. Though this was a common trend in European history,

158

Germany, especially Prussia, played a leading role. In Berlin, for example, even before the turn of the eighteenth century Jews had emerged from the ghetto and taken part in the formation of a modern urban society. This implied that emancipation also meant assimilation, integration into German culture, so that soon many families were regarded and even considered themselves no longer just as Jews, but as Germans of Jewish origin. Former outsiders had become full members of the citizenry; Jews got elected as members of parliament, as heads of chambers of commerce. And although access to the civil service was still restricted, from the middle of the nineteenth century onwards there were the first Jewish judges and university professors. And even more impressive was the fact that Jews, with just 1 per cent of the Prussian population, accounted for more than 10 per cent of grammar school and university students; among the numerous German Nobel Prize winners up until 1933, nearly 30 per cent were of Jewish extraction. The history of the Jews in nineteenth-century Germany was a success story.

But soon, from the beginning of the last quarter of the nineteenth century, when the rapid modernization of the German economy and society in general and the Great Depression in particular began to affect large sections of the German people, the tide turned again and traditional hatred of the Jews was replaced by a new form of anti-Semitism, which now did not turn against outsiders on the fringe of society but against Jewish people with considerable economic and social power and influence.

This 'modern' anti-Semitism was not based on religious belief but on the belief in racial differences which, it was argued, stood in the way of any policy of assimilation. Though in its radical form it remained restricted to the political right-wing fringe until the end of the Wilhelmine Empire, yet an anti-Semitic keynote permeated through society as a whole; clubs and student societies, for example, closed their ranks and no longer accepted Jews as members. Slowly the ground was prepared for the rabid anti-Semitism of Hitler and his executioners.

And it was Hitler with his pathological world-view, which he intended to realize with fanatical determination, who played the decisive role in the genesis of the 'Final Solution'. Without any doubt, the premeditated mass murder was the consummation of convictions and beliefs uttered early on in his *Mein Kampf*. And even before he started his war he had reaffirmed in the *Reichstag* on 30 January 1939 that the next war would result in the 'eradication of Judaism' from Europe – to destroy what he maintained was an international Jewish conspiracy against the natural superiority of the 'Aryan race'.

Of course, Hitler would never have been able to put his intentions into practice, to launch a huge and systematic campaign of racial genocide by means of modern industrial technology, without the co-operation of other fanatical anti-Semites and the complicity of a wide range of people and institutions, without whose support and active involvement it would not have been possible to organize a Europe-wide mass murder. The majority of willing executioners came from the SS, whose leader Heinrich Himmler, with his aides Reinhard Heydrich, Adolf Eichmann and many others, was finally responsible for the implementation of the Final Solution. But thousands more had to asssist in this gruesome task: police, civil servants, railway men and many others.

Officially the policy of extermination was classified 'top secret' and considerable care was taken to hide the grisly mass murdering in the killing centres located in remote areas of the occupied East. But, nevertheless, many thousands of Germans knew and millions more might have guessed the truth. Only a few tried to help, risking their lives by hiding Jewish friends. But most ignored the horror, not only because it concerned 'just Jews' but mainly because they were concerned with their own problems of daily survival in times of total war.

But by the time this concept of 'total war' was formally proclaimed by Goebbels in February 1943, the war had already been lost. After the German army had failed to complete a successful *Blitzkrieg* in the East by December 1941, and after war had also been declared on the USA, the crushing defeat of the Germans at Stalingrad between November 1942 and February 1943 and the surrender of the last German troops in Northern Africa marked the final turning points. From now on Hitler's armies were on the retreat, particularly after the successful Allied landings on the French coast in June 1944.

But long before the war was carried on to German territory at the end of this year, German civilians had already been involved through the constant effective bombing of German cities by British and American air forces. Those relentless attacks, which culminated in the bombing of Dresden in February 1945, when more than 120,000 fell victim to the resultant firestorm, were not only aimed at the destruction of the centres of the German armament industry but were also a futile attempt to crush the spirit of the civilian population, which glumly and passively endured the mounting devastation.

Yet, from 1933 onwards there had also been resistance to the regime, mostly isolated acts of sabotage by small left-wing groups or protests by courageous individuals from all political camps and segments of society – but it had never been really effective and had always been crushed ruthlessly. The only real threat to Hitler finally came from the conservative camp which had formerly eased his way to power. When a group of leading officers and administrators tried to assassinate Hitler on 20 July 1944, Hitler was lucky to survive the blast of the bomb placed under his table. Though no shadow of doubt can be cast on the moral integrity of those involved, their immediate motive had not been primarily the criminal nature of the regime but rather the imminent threat to the German nation-state which the demand of unconditional surrender implied, as it was first expressed at the conference of the Allies at Casablanca in January 1943. When Hitler took terrible revenge on the plotters, they died not for republicanism or democracy, but for law and justice and decency and, above all, for the future of the German nation-state.

At the same time, paradoxically, Germany was fortunate that the plot against Hitler failed. Of course, this meant more terror and war until the total collapse; however, if the plotters had succeeded, in the wake of inevitable defeat their success might only have given rise to another stab-in-the-back myth for German nationalists. Instead, it was important that Hitler lived long enough to assume complete responsibility for the final catastrophe. On 30 April 1945, after he had ordered the Germans never to surrender and proclaimed a 'scorched earth' policy, in a cowardly fashion he took his own life. A week later the German forces surrendered unconditionally and Hitler's Germany, the *Reich* which was meant to dominate Europe for the next thousand years, had ceased to exist.

Altogether, more than 55 million people, among them 25 million civilians, had lost their lives through war, terror and genocide. At the same time, the war unleashed by Nazi Germany had hastened the decline of Europe's leading role in world politics and helped to establish the USA and the Soviet Union as the leading world powers.

10

Two Germanies

UNDER ALLIED OCCUPATION AND PARTITION

Apart from the fact that the crimes committed by Nazi Germany attached a weight of moral guilt to the German name that has lasted to the present day, the most important legacy of Hitler's regime was the immediate consequence of total defeat which made 1945 another decisive turning point in the course of German history. For the time being, the end of Hitler's Germany also marked the end of the German nation-state. And Hitler had not only undone Bismarck's achievement but also gambled away the heartlands of this nineteenth-century *Reich*, because the Allied victors, determined to eradicate German militarism and authoritarianism, formally abolished Prussia by decree on 25 February 1947.

Moreover, nearly every German family was severely affected by the war and its outcome. Four million soldiers and 3.8 million civilians had been killed and many more had been crippled or their health had been affected by disease for the rest of their lives. Millions lived among ruins and rubble in the larger cities like Cologne, Hamburg or Frankfurt, which had been wrecked by carpet bombing, some in parts virtually obliterated. About eight million Germans from the eastern provinces of the *Reich* had either fled westwards before the end of the fighting or were driven from their homes after 1945.

Total victory at the end of a total war meant that there no longer existed a German state with which to negotiate any terms of peace: the Germans were totally at the mercy of the victorious Allied powers.

At a conference in Tehran in autumn 1943 the 'Big Three' (Russia, Britain and the USA) had already considered whether to dismember Germany altogether in order to eliminate it as a future factor in power politics. No definite decision was taken, but it was already decided that the Soviet Union was to retain that part of Poland it had occupied under the German–Soviet Pact of 1939, which meant that Poland was to be compensated with German territory in the west. This implied that roughly 25 per cent of the area of the *Reich* was placed under Soviet or Polish administration. There were also drafts of future zones of occupation and here as well as at Yalta (February 1945) general agreement was reached on the need for the demilitarization, denazification, decartellization and democratization of Germany.

Yet, it soon became evident that the Allies, although they agreed on how to deal with the German past, failed to reach agreement on the future structure of Germany. Their sense of unity crumbled when in the eyes of the Western Allies the German threat was supplanted by the rising threat of Soviet expansionism. Instead, with the alliance falling apart, the victors soon settled in their respective zones of occupation: the Russians in the east, the British in the north-west, the Americans in the south, the French in the south-west, and all four in Berlin. And in the wake of growing tensions between Stalin's Soviet Union and the USA and her Western allies, the history of Germany became part of the history of the Cold War.

Throughout the second half of the twentieth century the course of German history was determined by a system of world politics without Germany ever being able to play an active part in the ensuing gamble for world-wide hegemony. But in the end Germany obtained enormous benefit from this passive role: only 50 years after the end of a war which had left it on the brink of total extinction it had regained a leading place among the nation-states of Europe.

But in the beginning was the partition of Germany. After the American President Harry S. Truman, in a speech before both Houses of Congress on 12 March 1947, had made the 'containment of communism' the guiding principle of American foreign policy, it soon became evident that those parts of Germany which formed the zones of occupation of the Western powers could serve as an outpost in the system of defence against what was seen as the tide of Soviet expansionism. Just as the Russians soon started to turn their zone into a part of their general sphere of influence in Eastern Europe, so the Western powers set about integrating their zones into the Western political and economic orbit.

In 1948 it became evident that four-power co-operation had broken down and the establishment of two separate German political units

Map 9 Occupied Germany, 1945 (adapted from Dietrich Orlow, *A History of Modern Germany, 1971 to the Present* (Englewood Cliffs, NJ, 1987, p. 253).

was imminent. In a last-ditch effort Stalin tried to prevent the growing integration of Germany's Western zones and subjected West Berlin to a full-scale blockade. But the Western powers won their first victory in the Cold War, when they succeeded in supplying a city of two million people with everything that was needed via a huge airlift.

When in May 1949 the Soviets had to recognize their defeat and lifted the blockade, preparations for the creation of a separate West German Republic were well under way. And though the practical influence of Germans themselves on the flow of events was minimal, hardly anyone in the Western zones remained convinced that national unity was worth the price of Russian domination. When facing the blockade, Ernst Reuter, the newly elected Mayor of West Berlin argued: 'The division of Germany is not being created; it is a fact'.

The week the blockade ended, a new constitution, called 'Basic Law', was approved by the Western Military Governors, and the Western zones of occupation became the Federal Republic of Germany (FRG). Elections were held in August 1949 for the first parliament of the new state, which was to assemble at its new capital at Bonn, a small town on the banks of the Rhine. Though supreme authority continued to be vested in the three Western powers, the people of Western Germany now had the opportunity to conduct their own affairs within the limits set by the general framework of Western policy in the age of the Cold War. 'In other words, West Germany was to become a self-governing dominion under Allied supervision.'[1]

The Soviets responded in kind. When they realized that Germany as a whole could neither become part of their sphere of influence nor even be neutralized, they set up another German state as their puppet regime by founding the German Democratic Republic (GDR). The new state was officially proclaimed on 7 October 1949 with (East) Berlin as its capital.

From now on there were two German states, not just side by side but rather set against each other, because both Germanies were positioned in the van of opposing and even hostile political systems. They were not separated by a frontier in the way the Austrians and the Germans had been separated between 1866 and 1937, for example, but it was the 'Iron Curtain' which went down between the FGR and the GDR and at the same time divided Europe from the Baltic to the Mediterranean, and which was soon turned by the Eastern German regime into a fortified barrier. Each German state was firmly integrated into its respective bloc – the FRG as loyal ally of the United States, the GDR as the most obedient Soviet satellite.

To the extent to which each of the two Germanies strove to prove its trustworthiness towards its respective superpower, they succeeded in being accepted as equal partners within their alliance. In 1954 the GDR was recognized as a sovereign state by the Soviet Union and in the following year the FRG was granted full sovereignty. But these similarities should not obscure some fundamental differences in the relations of the two Germanies with their respective allies. Throughout its existence a sovereign GDR still depended on the presence of Russian troops, as had already become evident when, in 1953, Soviet tanks crushed a full-scale political uprising of the people who were demanding free elections, parliamentary democracy and reunification with West Germany.

THE FEDERAL REPUBLIC – POLITICAL STABILITY

In the West, the FRG achieved sovereignty only in exchange for a firm and lasting commitment to the anti-communist alliance led by the USA. But this policy, tenaciously pursued by its first Chancellor, Konrad Adenauer, could always rely on substantial public support, as repeated election victories of the government showed. Even when gaining the status of an equal partner meant rearmament and the introduction of national military service less than a decade after the end of the Second World War, this highly controversial issue did not endanger Adenauer's parliamentary majority. Obviously, there was no alternative to this policy as long as people preferred security and prosperity to vague Russian proposals concerning the restoration of German unity through the demilitarization of the country. Instead, Western Germany was admitted into the Western defence organization of NATO and at the same time the FRG formally became a sovereign nation, able to conduct its own foreign policy. Allied troops remained stationed on West German soil, now no longer as occupiers, but as allies and protectors.

Trying to recover the status of fully-fledged states thus implied that, placed in the front line of the East–West confrontation, each Germany had to regard the other Germany as its potential enemy. Yet, partition and confrontation in the sphere of politics did not correspond to the simple facts of life: there was hardly a German family that did not have relatives or friends on the other side of the Iron Curtain. As neither of the two German states had come into being primarily through the initiative of the German people, it was an open question whether or when the existence of two Germanies would destroy the unity of the German nation because, obviously, both new states were soon drifting apart. Not only did they belong to different political alliances, but they developed not just different but opposite political and economic systems which, in the long run, would generate different life-styles and mentalities.

In the West, the new constitution combined Germany's own pre-Nazi political traditions with the essentials of Western liberalism and parliamentary democracy. And here the authors of this Basic Law mainly drew upon the constitution of the Weimar Republic, not just as a model, but also to learn from its unfortunate history. Among other safeguards against the instability of governments as experienced during the Weimar era, a so-called '5 per cent hurdle' was introduced in order to keep fringe parties out of parliament. And this time the powers of the Federal President were reduced to mainly ceremonial functions. In accordance with the intentions of the Allies, who had already dismembered Prussia, a strong element of federalism was introduced as a balance between the political centre and the constituent parts of the Republic; the *Länder* were to be in charge of the administration and a substantial part of parliamentary legislation had to be approved of by an assembly of their delegates.

But when, indeed, Bonn did not become 'a second Weimar', this was due not so much to constitutional provisions and technicalities but to the fact that conditions for state building in 1949 were more favourable than in 1919. One reason was the fact that total defeat had left no room for a second national 'stab-in-the-back' myth. And this time the problem of negotiating a humiliating peace did not arise, because in the time of the Cold War the victors could not agree on a final settlement over Germany. Moreover, the harsh times of post-war misery and austerity were over when the FRG was founded, as was demonstrated by the end of food rationing by the end of 1949.

And this time the majority of the political class did not turn against democracy as they had done during the Weimar Republic, when it had been left to the Social Democrats and a minority of the Liberals to defend the constitution. After 1945 German Conservatives no longer opposed the parliamentary system; instead they became an integral part of Western German democracy. Once political parties were allowed to organize themselves in the Western zones in September 1945, besides the old parties of the Weimar era, like the SPD and the Communists, a new party, the *Christlich Demokratische Union* (CDU) soon established itself as a major political force. It was a merger between the old Catholic Centre Party and the representatives of Protestant German Conservatism. And under the leadership of Konrad Adenauer, born in 1876 and a prominent member of the old Centre Party, it was mainly the CDU which finally won over the German middle classes to parliamentary democracy. This marked a decisive watershed in German history because from now on democracy was rooted in the majority of the German electorate. In contrast to the era of the Weimar Republic, no formidable right-wing anti-parliamentarian movement has yet managed to estabish itself.

The price to be paid for a high degree of political stability was a certain amount of continuity between the FRG and the times before 1945. Whereas the constitution of the new Western German state looked back to the democratic revolutions of 1848 and 1919, those who actually ran the new state were to a considerable extent those who had served under the Nazi regime – in spite of the fact that the Allied victors initially had put denazification high on their agenda.

Though between November 1945 and the following October, 24 of Hitler's high officials were tried and 11 sentenced to death by an International Military Tribunal at Nuremberg, denazification on a comprehensive scale was to prove extremely difficult, inconclusive and in many cases simply unfair. By the end of 1945 about 140,000 people had been arrested in the Western Zones and hundreds of thousands were removed from office or had work applications refused. And though millions had been obliged to fill out special questionnaires and had been examined by special tribunals, when procedures were finally stopped by 1 January 1949 the purge had failed to achieve its ambitious goal. Opinion polls carried out by the American Military Government showed that in 1948 more than 50 per cent of the Germans still thought that National Socialism had been a good idea, but badly executed, and even in 1951 47 per cent judged the years between 1933 and 1939 to have been Germany's best years of the twentieth century.[2]

In May 1951 the parliament of the FRG, the *Bundestag*, passed a law reinstating 150,000 civil servants who had formerly lost their positions in the process of denazification. In the higher echelons of the federal ministries about 50 per cent of the staff (even more in the Foreign Office) were former members of the NSDAP, and not a single judge, not even those who had served in Hitler's notorious 'People's Court', was tried and condemned for his activities during the 'Third Reich'. The ex-NSDAP member Theodor Oberländer became Minister for Refugees in Adenauer's second Cabinet and the CDU politician Kurt Georg Kiesinger, Chancellor from 1966 to 1969, had once worked for Goebbels' world radio service.

This obvious degree of continuity did not imply that the FRG was Hitler's Germany resurrected. The great majority of those now in office again, who had been involved with Hitler's movement, had not been fanatical Nazis, but had been critics or even enemies of the Weimar democracy and had put their service at the disposal of the dictator, or had just been fellow-travellers in order to further their professional career. Moreover, the new republic badly needed expertise, especially in the fields of administration, jurisprudence and education and soon also in the military sector as well. Against the background of the Cold War anti-communism overshadowed any efforts to deal critically and effectively with the Nazi past.

At the same time, this development provided an important element of stability because it contributed decisively to reconciling to the new democracy large sectors of middle- and upper-class Germany which were still attached to conservative traditions reaching back to Bismarck's Germany and which, in fact, had supported Hitler. 'If parliamentary democracy was the only state form on offer which could protect them against "bolshevism", most of them were willing to work with it.'[3] During the long period of Adenauer's governments (1949–63) they even learnt that the parliamentary system allowed them to enjoy the fruits of political power. Against all expectations, until 1972 the SPD never managed to win a majority at general elections but always came second to the CDU which, in 1957, even won an overall majority of 52 per cent.

In the beginning, the CDU achieved this by a staunch anti-communism which, in a way, replaced the ardent nationalism of former times and which was combined with social conservatism tempered by elements of Christian Socialism. Later on, it would reap the benefits of Adenauer's policy which offered protection from the communist threat and at the same time prosperity for everyone, so that until well into the 1960s the CDU was on the way to becoming the natural governing party of the FRG; only once, in the elections of 1972, did it not become the strongest party. And only once did a chancellor lose office as the direct result of a general election as did Kiesinger (CDU) in 1969; the next major change in government, which brought back the CDU into office in 1982, was effected by the small liberal party, the FDP, changing coalition partners.

It took some time for democracy to become firmly rooted in West German political culture and in this process the year 1969 marked a decisive moment, because from now on, for a period of 13 years, governments did not include the CDU and the Germans learned that a working democracy implies a change in the assigning of the roles of government and opposition.

The new administration headed by the charismatic SPD leader Willy Brandt took office in a period of general change and even world-wide turmoil, which also affected the FRG. These were the years of protest against the American intervention in Vietnam and of general challenge to the received wisdom of the Adenauer era, its single-minded anti-communism and its apologetic attitudes with regard to pre-1945 Germany. For the first time since the turbulent Weimar years the people of Western Germany witnessed mass demonstrations, often bordering on violent action, organized by an extraparliamentary opposition (APO), whose hard core was formed by representatives of a new generation of students. Led by students, Germany took part in the '68 revolution, which effected deep and long-lasting cultural change. But again Bonn was not Weimar. The new democracy weathered the storm, this time blowing from the left. Apart from a small core of fanatics who drifted into terrorism, the APO by and by adapted to the principles and rules of parliamentary democracy when it was either absorbed by the SPD or provided the basis for a new Green Party.

All things considered, West German democracy proved to be in good working order and Germans, for the first time in history, enjoyed political stability and political freedom at the same time.

THE FEDERAL REPUBLIC – ECONOMIC PROSPERITY

The solid basis for this long period of stability was provided by the spectacular success of the West German economy, by what soon was called the 'economic miracle': a period of rapid and sustained economic growth which, in the span of only 20 years, turned the FRG into a prosperous, even affluent society of the Western world. And again, at the beginning of this dramatic recovery there were the consequences of the Cold War. As soon as the Americans realized that they needed West Germany as a vital base against the communist threat, they decided to include Germany in their 'European Recovery Programme', usually called the Marshall Plan, launched in June 1947. With a courageous currency reform and the decision for a free market economy with the virtual elimination of all controls and forms of rationing, the stage had been set for the West German 'economic miracle' in 1948, even before the foundation of the Federal Republic. But it was also an important step towards the final partition of the country, binding the Western zones closely to the Western world, which was moving into position for the Cold War.

In view of the vast devastation caused by wartime bombing, the acute housing shortage, the breakdown of the transport system, the millions of refugees and expellees, the task of reconstruction was more than formidable. But the collapse also provided opportunities for modernization and structural modifications. The enormous extent of the rebuilding effort also meant that for many years there would be a huge market for a wide range of products and, due to the fact that the population of West Germany was 20 per cent larger than before the war, economic development would not be held back by a shortage of labour.

Under these conditions and with an overall American backing, Ludwig Erhard, Economics Minister in the Adenauer government, argued that a relatively unfettered market economy would provide the greatest amount of prosperity for the greatest number of West Germans. And indeed, during the boom period between 1951 and 1963 gross domestic product rose by an annual rate of 8 per cent, the disposable income of the average German family by 400 per cent between 1950 and 1970 and unemployment sank from 9.1 per cent in 1951 to 0.7 per cent in 1962, while the annual rate of inflation fluctuated around 2 per cent. At the same time Germany was on the way to become one of the world's leading exporters. Only Japan, the other great power which had lost the war, could exceed the German economic achievement in this period.

Economic success had, of course, important political repercussions. For all its benefits, the free market economy in absolute terms widened the gap between the rich and the poor; but it was widely accepted mainly because after such a time of dearth and misery it now provided major increases in the standard of living for virtually everybody. It was also flanked by comprehensive social welfare projects, including special measures to equalize the burdens of the lost war among the German population. Under a law of 1952 partial compensation for war-related losses was granted which mainly benefited the refugees and thereby contributed to their successful integration into West German society.

But most important for the general acceptance of a free market-society was to mitigate its effects – the aggravating uneven distribution of private wealth – by proclaiming the model of a 'social market economy' as the guiding principle of official economic and social policy. In fact, the Adenauer governments built on a tradition of social policy which reached back not just to the Weimar Republic but to

Bismarck's Germany. With the law of 1957, which index-linked substantially subsidized pensions to the cost of living, the welfare state was to supplement the free market economy. Its underlying idea was to set solidarity between the generations against unbridled competition between individuals, because from now on one generation in work would pay for the previous one.

Finally, laissez-faire capitalism in Germany was to some extent curbed by strong federal trade unions that were granted by law not just the right to negotiate wages but also a certain amount of co-determination concerning mainly the social consequences of the commercial operations of firms and companies.

On the whole, such policies worked extremely well during the boom period with its outstanding growth rates, and compared to her European neighbours Germany's economy was very little hampered by major strikes or other social conflicts.

Another important consequence of West Germany's economic success story was the SPD's turn towards a more pragmatic and liberal economic policy. Originally, the party had opposed Erhard's plan for economic recovery because it was based on the principles of private ownership and the rule of capitalism. Instead, until the middle of the 1950s Social Democrats advocated a centrally planned economy with public ownership of basic industries and natural resources. Against an economy which was in fact widening the gap between the few rich and the masses of the less well off they wanted to set up an equitable system of income distribution. But under the influence of the overwhelming electoral success of Adenauer's government in the 1953 and 1957 general elections, the party in November 1959 adopted the Godesberg Programme, which distanced the German SPD from the fundamental tenets of Marxism. Planned economy was now rejected in favour of the adoption of the principles of the social market economy. This obvious swing to a Western orientation was an important condition for future success at the polls.

The period of the 'economic miracle' was also a period of fundamental changes within the economic and social framework of the Western part of Germany. Whereas between 1882 and 1939 the percentage of those working in the agrarian sector of the economy had gradually declined from 43 per cent to 25 per cent, it now fell from 23 per cent to only 3 per cent during the relatively short span of less than 40 years between 1950 and 1987. This was mainly the result of a process of rigorous modernization and concentration of agrarian production, which forced the majority of small farmers to give up. At the same time, those farmers and agrarian entrepreneurs who stayed in business managed to exert disproportionately strong political influence by skilful lobbying as a pressure group within the CDU. The result was that up to the present day German farmers have profited from a system of agricultural protection und subvention which guarantees them prices well above the level of the world food market.

With the end of the war the special role of the German aristocracy had also come to an end; in particular the Prussian gentry had lost its dominating influence in certain fields such as the army and the higher civil service. After 1945 their landed estates, which had formed the economic basis of their position, either fell victim to the loss of Germany's eastern provinces or to the land reform in the Soviet zone. Now members of the nobility who in Weimar Germany had still determinedly opposed and obstructed democracy, no longer exerted any palpable political influence.

All in all, in the course of the short history of the Federal Republic traditional social differences were levelled down. At the lower end of the scale parts of the traditional working class were merged into a larger middle class consisting of skilled blue- and white-collar workers, technicians and civil servants. At the same time a high degree of horizontal mobility had important long-range effects on the social structure: millions of refugees and expellees, as well as those moving from the countryside into the urban centres, caused a more heterogeneous population mix. Traditional regional barriers became more or less obsolete, and even the differences which had separated Catholics and Protestants for so many centuries were partly reduced. Compared to the *Reich* this society proved to be much more homogeneous. Though private wealth was in fact most unevenly spread, most West Germans were firmly convinced of being members of a classless society or, at least, of a society where everybody possesses the same chance to rise to the top.

All in all, as an outpost of the Western camp in the Cold War, the FRG became the showcase for an affluent, consumer-oriented society, and this prosperity was its chief asset in its rivalry with the other Germany.

THE GERMAN DEMOCRATIC REPUBLIC

Whereas the FRG soon profited from the consequences of the partition of Germany, for the Eastern zonethis division meant that it had to bear the brunt of defeat. And whereas in the face of the devastated condition of the German economy in 1945 the Western Allies soon abandoned all their original plans concerning reparations and structural reform like 'decartellization' of German industry, the Russians pursued these original goals unrelentingly. Until the end of 1946, more than 1000 plants had been dismantled in the Eastern zone and transferred to the Soviet Union; and until 1953 the East German economy was burdened with debt the equivalent of 14 billion dollars: 'It was the East Germans who paid the full price for Hitler's war', wrote a West German columnist in 1985.[4]

At the same time the Russians, guided by the conviction that Nazism had been essentially the product of 'monopoly capitalism', set out to destroy the basis of capitalism by taking over immediate control of all banks and major manufacturing industries, and a systematic land reform programme ordered the expropriation and break-up of all larger estates. The land was turned into smaller holdings and given to half a million agricultural workers and small peasants (who, from 1952 onwards, would later be compelled to join Agricultural Production Co-operatives or other forms of collective farms). By the beginning of 1946 in Eastern Germany the old German economic elite had been stripped of its power and property.

For the Russians, the foundation of a socialist society depended on thorough denazification. Indeed, up to August 1947 more than 16,000 members of the SS, the secret police and the higher ranks of the NSDAP were brought to court and more than 12,000 sentenced (118 were sentenced to death). Such rigorous measures, which mainly affected the public sector, helped to make room for Communist Party members in key positions in the civil service, the police and the judiciary, since from the very beginning the Soviet Military Administration for Germany pursued the goal of laying the foundations for a future communist society, at least in their Eastern zone of occupation.

In this game the Russians set their hopes on the reputation of the Communist party as the most determined former opponent of Hitler's regime. In April 1945, a group of German Communist leaders who had spent the war years in Russia were brought back, now resolved to complete the socialist revolution that had failed in Germany in 1919. But their party was soon identified with the ruthless policy of the Soviet Military Government, so when the Communists realized that they would never be able to gain victory in a free election, their greatest rival, the SPD, was forced into a fusion with the KPD. On 22 April 1946 the Socialist Unity Party (SED) came into being in the Soviet zone and was to continue the policy of the KPD in a new guise.

Thus, when in the wake of the foundation of the FGR the GDR was established, it was organized along the lines of the political structure of the USSR. Though the East German Constitution appeared to be as democratic as the Basic Law of the FRG – as it also resembled in many aspects that of the Weimar Republic – in fact the political system in East Germany amounted to a one-party rule by the SED, which set up a puppet regime of Stalin's Russia. And just as this state was controlled by the SED, so this party was not organized along the lines of party democracy but was ruthlessly and efficiently controlled from above. Ultimate decisions were taken by the party leadership; the first secretary of the SED, whose office was not even mentioned by the constitution, was in fact the most powerful person: Walter Ulbricht from 1950 to 1971 and then Erich Honnecker until the fall of the regime in 1989.

Although Communists in East Germany proclaimed the dawn of a new Socialist Germany, here, too, there were still many links to the past. The new political leaders had been persecuted by the Nazis and anti-fascism became the guiding political principle of the GDR, but there is no denying the fact that here people lived – 'notwithstanding substantial ethical differences'[5] – under conditions similar to those of Hitler's Germany: a dictatorship in the form of a one-party system, repressing all forms of political opposition, controlling public opinion and putting pressure on everyone to conform to the standards of socialism as it was defined by official party ideology.

Yet, it was not so much the lack of political freedom, which East Germans had not experienced since 1933, but the poor performance of the economy which was of serious consequence for the future history of the GDR. Hampered by often absurd planning priorities and a cumbersome bureaucracy, the centralized economy constantly failed the expectations of the people, though in fact East Germany soon far outstripped its Communist allies in Eastern Europe, including the Soviet Union, in the fields of productivity and standard of living. In spite of its initial difficulties – the lack of raw materials and the costs of the reparations – the GDR could present impressive figures of annual growth varying between 5 per cent and 8 per cent towards the end of the 1950s. And after the 1953 uprising the Party even decided to increase the supply of consumer goods.

Yet, every economic success in the GDR was clouded by the long shadow cast by the economic miracle of the FRG because people in the East were always looking towards the West, stunned by the obvious prosperity of their 'brothers and sisters' living beyond the river Elbe. Despite all economic efforts and achievements, productivity and the standard of living in East Germany always remained substantially below that of the Federal Republic.

Economic failure lay at the root of general dissatisfaction and as people had no opportunity to utter criticism or even organize opposition, they 'voted with their feet' against the SED regime. Between 1949 and 1961 about 2.75 million East Germans moved permanently to West Germany. And as nearly half of those refugees were under 25 years of age, the GDR was losing an essential segment of its workforce. The loophole in the Iron Curtain for such a massive exodus was offered by Berlin. And when in 1961 the stream of refugees in April alone rose to 30,000, the regime realized that this haemorrhage had to be stopped at all costs. With the support of the Soviet Union, and at the price of another severe international crisis, in August 1961 this last escape route to the West was closed by 'the Wall', a huge concrete barrier separating East from West Berlin and preventing uncontrolled travel between the two halves of the city. From now on the population of the GDR was completely fenced in by their government. Anyone who tried to leave the country would risk his life and, indeed, by 1989 235 people had been shot in their attempt to cross the Wall.

This barrier was testimony to the fact that the East German regime had failed to win the consent of its own people and therefore had to take them prisoners, and it proved to the world that there were two Germanies, set against each other and growing more and more apart. From now on East Germans no longer had any choice but to accept the reality of their country and to find ways of coming to terms with the rule of the SED.

Thus, less than two decades after the end of the war diverging societies were developing in East and West Germany. At the root of this was the difference between two economic systems. Whereas in the West capital remained predominantly in private ownership, more than 95 per cent of the workforce in the East were engaged in state-owned enterprises or similar forms of collectivized production. Wages were lower than in the West but there was no risk of unemployment. And though certain people, especially members of the political elite, possessed considerable privileges, these were seldom enjoyed in public and there were fewer people with high incomes in the East than in the West, where disparity between the top and the bottom of the social scale was far greater.

Efforts to develop a more egalitarian society went together with a policy to improve the position of women. Legal equality of women was achieved earlier than in the FRG and in the 1980s 50 per cent of the East German workforce was female compared with 39 per cent in West Germany. And as the majority of children who needed a place in a kindergarten were provided for, nearly 75 per cent of mothers of two children were working full time, even though many might have preferred to stay at home.

As in the West, the GDR, too, followed the established German tradition of comprehensive social policies in return for political loyalty, when the concept of a cradle-to-grave welfare state was put on the agenda. In order to guarantee the necessities of life for everyone – a work-place, basic foodstuffs like bread and potatoes, housing and local transportation – heavy public subsidies, amounting to a quarter of the state budget were required, often with disastrous consequences for the economy as a whole – when, for example, pigs were sometimes fed with bread, which was cheaper than fodder. In the late 1980s this kind of policy heavily contributed to the fact that the GDR's state finances were on the brink of bankruptcy.

All in all, the regime's attempts to create a more egalitarian society failed because citizens kept looking to the West, realizing that this kind of social equality meant less freedom of choice and a lower standard of living. Still, it provided social conditions and profiles which made East Germans develop life-styles, expectations and patterns of behaviour quite different from those in the West.

FROM SEPARATION TO UNIFICATION

As the two Germanies grew slowly apart, the GDR gradually succeeded in becoming a recognized member on the stage of international politics. This was achieved despite tenacious resistance from the FRG. Because of their exposed positions in the systems of antagonistic Cold War politics, both German governments propagated contradictory self-images. From the outset the FRG had claimed to be the sole heir to the German Reich and the unification of Germany was enshrined in the preamble of its Constitution as its main foreign policy goal. This implied that the 'so-called GDR' was in fact the 'Soviet Zone of Occupation', where the government did not represent the people and which for that reason should not be recognized as a state in its own right. According to this doctrine, enunciated by Adenauer's government in 1955, the FRG would instantly break off diplomatic relations with countries recognizing the GDR. With the support of the USA a barrier was erected which limited the GDR's diplomatic ties to the sphere of Communist regimes.

This rigid West German attitude towards the other Germany became obsolete when towards the end of the 1960s the Western Powers aimed at a relaxation of tensions with the Soviet bloc. Germany did not stay aloof from such a development when, under the leadership of the SPD Chancellor Willy Brandt, relations with Communist countries in general and the GDR in particular were transformed by a new foreign policy referred to as *Ostpolitik*.

By easing tensions through the 'normalization' of relations between the two Germanies the new government intended to work towards a situation which might even lead to some form of unification or association of the two parts. In 1973, in the so-called Basic Treaty, the FRG conceded that there were 'two German states in one German nation', though in spite of such a *de facto* recognition of the GDR by the Bonn government it still refused to regard the GDR as a completely foreign state. In the same year both Germanies were simultaneously accepted as members of the United Nations. Finally, the climax of this process of 'normalization' was reached when in September 1987 Erich Honnecker, First Secretary of the SED and Head of the State Council of the GDR, was received by the West German Chancellor Helmut Kohl (CDU) in Bonn on the occasion of a formal state visit. And although the West German government stressed that it did not accept the Wall in Berlin, it obviously accepted the fact of the side-by-side existence of two Germanies for many years to come.

Only two years later the Wall came down, the GDR simply evaporated and the way was free for the two Germanies to reunite. And again, just as the partition of Germany between 1945 and 1949 was the result of the general development of world politics, so the reunification of 1989/90 was also due to a rapid fundamental change of the international scene. Division was brought about by the outbreak of the Cold War; the rebirth of a unified German nation-state came with the end of the Cold War. And as both Germanies, up to the end of this period, had been firmly integrated into their respective bloc systems, and as the Cold War did not end in a draw but in a clear victory for the West which, in the end, had won an extended arms race, the Federal Republic was in a position to determine the conditions of reunification.

The pivotal trigger for a huge chain reaction was the election of Mikhail Gorbachev as First Secretary of the Russian Communist Party. As the first Soviet leader to be untainted by a Stalinist record, he soon embarked on a course of radical reforms, which also encouraged fundamental political change in other Eastern European states, because now Moscow no longer insisted that no communist state could ever be allowed to escape from the Soviet orbit. And, indeed, in the summer of 1989 a new reformist government replaced communist hardliners in Hungary and partly free elections took place in Poland. These developments had severe implications for the GDR because it became evident that nearly 30 years of outward stability had only thinly veiled the fact that the SED regime had never been able to gain the support of the majority of the East Germans. For as soon as Hungary dismantled her part of the 'Iron Curtain' frontier, 40,000 GDR citizens moved via Hungary and Austria to West Germany within a few weeks; the exodus of the 1950s was revived.

At the same time, criticism and discontent were being voiced openly within the GDR, where Protestant churches – for example in Leipzig – became starting points for impressive demonstrations, demanding freedom to travel and proclaiming the slogan 'We are the people'. Courageous individuals began to organize platforms for the discussion of political reform. And when Mikhail Gorbachev visited the GDR on the occasion of her 40th anniversary, he commented on the need for reform with the remark that 'life punishes those who come too late'. After such clear signals the regime did not dare to use force against the rapidly growing mass of demonstrators. On 16 October about 100,000 gathered on the streets of Leipzig, and two days later Honnecker was pressured into resignation. On 4 November more than half a million people demonstrated for freedom in East Berlin, on 9 November jubilant Berliners from the east and the west streamed through the opened checkpoints or even climbed the wall and began to hack it down. Now the SED was fast losing its grip – in December the Party gave up its monopoly on power and finally free elections were fixed for 18 March 1990.

For the first time in history Germans had successfully completed their revolution. And it was equally remarkable that this was a 'velvet revolution' – a revolution without blood being shed. The big difference between the rising of 1953 and the revolution of 1989 was that this time the Russian tanks stayed in their camps and the Russian soldiers remained in their barracks. And so, in the end, it was evident that the communist regime in the GDR had always ultimately been based on the protecting power of the Soviet Union.

The opening of the border and the prospect of democratic freedom did not put an end to the rallies in the streets; instead it led to a change in the agenda. The slogan 'We are the people' was altered to: 'We are one people'. This cry for unification with the West did not echo pan-German national instincts, but expressed the wish to gain prosperity as well as freedom. Once the Wall had come down and the gates to earthly paradise were thrown wide open people wished to enter it for good. And again they voted with their feet – this time it was not against a repressive regime but against the drab reality of what was called 'real existing socialism'. The exodus to the West continued, rapidly exacerbating a situation in which the GDR was disintegrating and the FRG threatened and burdened with the massive influx of more than 2000 people a day seeking to settle in West Germany. It now became obvious that the question was not 'whether' but 'when' and 'how' the two Germanies were to reunite.

At this point the centre of initiative shifted from the streets in East Germany to the West German government. Though throughout the last four decades Bonn had always paid lip service to the ultimate political goal of reunification, it was now taken by surprise. And it had to be cautious in its approach because of the firm integration of the FRG into the organizations of the Western Alliance, even more so as US President George Bush insisted on NATO membership of a reunited Germany. The big question was how to combine such a solution with the security interest of the Soviet Union, which would obviously prefer Germany to be a neutral power. And at the same time France and Britain were irritated by the prospect of a united German nation-state again dominating Central Europe.

In this situation it was West Germany's Chancellor Kohl who almost single-handedly achieved his goal: the reunification of Germany with the final assent of the former Allied Powers as well as all her neighbouring states. In this remarkable feat of diplomacy he could always rely on the support of the United States; four decades of unwavering loyalty of the FRG to the leading Western Power were now refunded. And Kohl was also assisted by Gorbachev, who realized that it would be futile to try to turn the tide. Already in mid-July the

Soviet Union acquiesced in the new Germany's membership of NATO in return for American willingness to balance the strategic losses for Russia by offers of greater security through disarmament and weapons control and by Germany granting substantial financial aid to the ailing Russian economy. During the summer of 1990 all problems concerning the international aspects of German reunification were solved by the so-called 'Two-plus-Four' negotiations between the four former Allies and the two Germanies. The result equated to a final peace treaty, when it confirmed the full sovereignty of a reunited Germany.

Negotiations concerning the domestic issues of unification were conducted with all the initiative being on the West German side, because the representatives of the newly elected GDR government were under pressure for rapid unification in order to prevent total chaos in the East. This circumstance was used by Kohl and his East German counterpart de Mazière as an argument against all plans for devising a new constitution by the representatives of the two Germanies. Instead, unification was to take place under the provisions of Article 23 of the West German Basic Law, stipulating that this Law would be in force in such parts of Germany as decided to enter the Federal Republic, which amounted to a take-over of East Germany by West Germany. The visions of those who had spearheaded the 'velvet revolution' and had dreamt of a renewed democratic socialism were swept away. When the East German negotiators tried to safeguard certain social achievements of the GDR, such as the right to work, they were soon outmanoeuvred by those from the West who, for example, refused to accept property ownership in East Germany as it stood on the day of unification and successfully insisted that former owners, who had fled to the West, should be enabled to present claims to property they had not occupied for decades, despite the fact that they had already received some form of compensation in the FRG.

In fact, the terms for the internal arrangements were more or less dictated by the West German government and its Chancellor Helmut Kohl, who always had an eye to the next general election, which was to be the first all-German free election since 1932. To buy the goodwill of the East Germans, a currency union was effected on 1 July 1990 which abolished the East German mark and replaced it at the favourable exchange rate of one to one by the West German D-Mark – with disastrous consequences for the tottering East German economy which was all of a sudden exposed to the strains and pitfalls of a free market – but with the effect that Helmut Kohl and his party could celebrate an overwhelming victory at the first pan-German general elections.

After monetary union political union became a mere formality: on 3 October 1990 Germans celebrated their reunification, when five reconstituted former East German *Länder* were incorporated into an enlarged FRG and a new chapter in the history of Germany opened up.

Epilogue: Today's Germany

The first German nation-state had been Prussia's Germany, according to the dominating political and military role this East German kingdom had played in the process of unification; in today's Germany the tables have been turned and the balance has shifted in favour of Western and Southern Germany because of the domineering economic role the former FRG played on the occasion of reunification. And it is still the economy that makes all the difference between East and West and stands in the way of turning mere incorporation into genuine assimilation of the two former Germanies.

'What belongs together now has to grow together', Willy Brandt, the former West German Chancellor, told his fellow countrymen the night the Wall came down. But when Chancellor Kohl's vision of 'blossoming landscapes' in the East turned sour, disappointment and scepticism replaced initial euphoria. The East German economy, whose efficiency and productivity had been grossly overrated, could not withstand the shock of abrupt transition to a market society. Industrial production shrank by 70 per cent between 1989 and 1992, by 1994 less than 8 per cent of the general domestic product came from the East; the result was mass unemployment and further migration to the West.

Even a decade after unification many East Germans still feel themselves to be the poor relatives of their wealthy brothers and sisters in the West. Moreover, certain aspects of the take-over by the West Germans helped to widen the gulf which still separates the two sides, because in some fields '*Wessies*'(as those from the West are called) treated '*Ossies*' in the way victors may deal with their defeated enemies. Contrary to the leniency shown towards many ex-Nazis during the first decades of the FRG, this time not only were the most prominent representatives of Communist Germany put on trial, but whole branches of public services and administration, especially in the fields of education, the media and the law, were purged of

183

former SED members and often also of harmless fellow travellers of the former regime.

But West Germans also had – and still have – to pay the price for unification. Though the economy in the West gained spectacular profits when the currency union unleashed a huge demand for Western consumer goods, it soon became evident that raising East Germany to the level of the West could not be left to market forces alone but required state intervention and financial aid on a large scale. Up to the present day, each year around 130 billion Deutschmarks have been transferred to the new *Länder* in the East, mostly provided by the tax-payers in the West. And as Chancellor Kohl had missed the opportunity for a serious appeal to his fellow countrymen to rise to the huge challenge which went with the task of reunification, for many Germans in both former Germanies irritation and disappointment have replaced the euphoria and optimism which characterized the hour of the rebirth of their nation-state. Instead of reunification forming a new corporate identity, there still exists an invisible wall separating '*Wessies*' from '*Ossies*'.

The burden of unifying and assimilating the two estranged parts of Germany considerably adds to the difficulties of present efforts to adapt Germany's economy and society to the consequences of general globalization. Today Germans find that it is becoming increasingly difficult to maintain an exceptionally high standard of living as well as a closely knit net of social security for everybody.

Yet, in spite of a relatively high rate of unemployment (around 10 per cent) the German economy is still the strongest in Europe. And, even more importantly, in spite of sometimes heated discussions about how to distribute stagnating or even shrinking national wealth in a more competitive world, the looming economic and social crisis has not generated a general political crisis. Of course, there is criticism of government policies, particularly by those who feel they are the victims of recent social reforms, but this does not degenerate into criticism of democracy. Neither on the left nor on the right of the political spectrum can any formidable gathering of the forces of political radicalism be observed.

And what is even more important is that there are no stirrings of a new or even violent nationalism. On the contrary: nearly all political parties agree that the regained German nation-state can only be secured as an integral part of a supra-national European Union. There was no change in German European policy after reunification and Germans even consented to abandon their cherished *Deutschmark* for the sake of European unity. Clearly, Germans have learnt their lesson from the last turbulent century of Germany's history.

Notes

CHAPTER 3. FROM THE REFORMATION TO THE THIRTY YEARS' WAR

1. *Luther's Works*, ed. J. Pelikan and H. T. Lehmann, Philadelphia, PA, 1955ff., vol. XLIV, p.142f.
2. *Luther's Works*, vol. XXXI, p. 37.
3. C. Scott Dixon, *The Reformation in Germany*, Oxford, 2002, p. 18.

CHAPTER 4. EIGHTEENTH-CENTURY GERMANY

1. F. C. von Moser, *Vom Deutschen Nationalgeist*, 1766, p. 5f.
2. H. Möller, *Fürstenstaat oder Bürgernation. Deutschland, 1763–1815*, Berlin, 1998, p. 56.

CHAPTER 5. REVOLUTION AND THE FORMATION OF THE NATION-STATE

1. Count Hardenberg, 12 September 1807, in *Die Reorganisation des preußischen Staates unter Stein und Hardenberg*, ed. George Winter, vol. 1 (Leipzig, 1931), p. 306.

CHAPTER 6. INDUSTRIALIZATION AND SOCIAL CHANGE

1. D. Blackbourn, *The Fontana History of Germany, 1780–1918*, London, 1997, p. 217.

CHAPTER 8. WEIMAR GERMANY

1. M. Fulbrook, *History of Germany, 1918–2000: The Divided Nation*, 1st edn, Oxford, 1991, p. 53.

CHAPTER 9. HITLER'S GERMANY

1. Adolf Hitler, *Mein Kampf*, English translation, Boston, MA, 1943, p. 654.
2. W. Hofer (ed.), *Der Nationalsozialismus, Dokumente 1933–45*, Frankfurt, 1957, p. 731.
3. Hans Ulrich Thamer, *Verführung und Gewalt: Deutschland, 1933–1945*, Berlin, 1986, p. 178.
4. M. Fulbrook, *History of Germany, 1918–2000: The Divided Nation*, 1st edn, Oxford, 1991, p. 85.
5. Fulbrook, *Divided Nation*, 1st edn, p. 105; R. Breitman, 'The Final Solution', in: G. Martel, *Modern Germany Reconsidered, 1870–1945*, London, 1992, p. 198.

CHAPTER 10. TWO GERMANIES

1. L. Kettenacker, *Germany since 1945*, Oxford, 1997, p. 38.
2. Gerhard A. Ritter, *Über Deutschland. Die Bundesrepublik in der deutschen Geschichte*, Munich, 1998, p. 122.
3. A. Nicholls, *The Bonn Republic: West German Democracy, 1945–1990*, Oxford, 1995, p. 110.
4. Nicholls, *The Bonn Republic*, p. 14.
5. Kettenacker, *Germany since 1945*, p. 217.

Chronology

58–51 BC	Caesar conquers Gaul; the frontier of the Roman Empire reaches the Rhine
38/50 BC	Roman foundation of Cologne
16–5 BC	Roman armies advance to the Danube. Foundation of Trier, Augsburg and Mainz
8 BC–AD 6	Roman efforts to conquer the lands between Rhine and Elbe
9	Decisive victory by Arminius over Roman army
84	Romans begin to construct the border fortification of the *limes* between Rhine and Danube
From 162	Repeated raids by Germanic tribes into Roman territory
Late 3rd century	Trier becomes one of the imperial Roman residences
From 313	Expansion of Christianity in Central Europe. Among other cities Cologne and Trier become bishoprics
From 375	Start of great Germanic migration
406	Romans abandon the Rhine as imperial frontier
476	End of Western Roman Empire
From 482	Rise of the kingdom of the Franks under the Merovingian dynasty (Hlodwig *c*.466–511)
6th century	On the one hand, expansion of Frankish rule in nearly all directions; on the other, frequent partitions of the realm (e.g. Neustria in the west, Austria in the east)
From 629	The Merovingian monarchs begin to lose control to the hereditary 'mayors of the palace', who soon form the Carolingian dynasty (Charles Martel 688–741)
From 719	Intensified missionary activity of Christian church among Germanic tribes (Bonifatius *c*.673–754)
732	Charles Martel's victory over the Arabs at Poitiers. Thenceforth the Muslims are held on the line of the Pyrenees

768–814	Reign of Charlemagne who again unites the empire of the Franks
773–4	Conquest of the kingdom of the Lombards
775–804	Conquest of Saxony
788	Conquest of Bavaria
800	Charlemagne crowned Emperor by Pope Leo
843	Treaty of Verdun: three-way partition of Carolingian Empire
870	Partition of the middle kingdom between the eastern and western Frankish kingdoms, which start to form the geographic cores of future Germany and France
895–955	Frequent raids by the Magyars, especially into the lands of the eastern kingdom
911	End of Carolingian dynasty in eastern Frankish kingdom
919–1024	Kings of the Saxon dynasty
936–73	Otto I (the Great)
936/37	Organization of the Marches as bases of defence and expansion towards Slav territory in the East
951	Otto establishes rule over the kingdom of Italy
955	Decisive victory over the Magyars in the battle of the Lechfield
962	Otto crowned emperor
967	Marriage between the future Otto II and the Byzantine princess Theophanu as the result of mutual recognition of both empires
1024–1125	Kings of the Salian dynasty
1033	Union of the Empire with the kingdom of Burgundy
1039–56	Reign of Henry III represents peak of imperial power. In 1046 he divests three popes
1056–1106	Henry IV
1059	Henceforth papal elections by the College of Cardinals shall assert independence of Papacy
1075	In his *Dictatus Papae* Pope Gregory VII claims supreme power within Christendom. Start of the Investiture Contest. Henry defeats rebellious Saxons
1077	Canossa – Henry IV succeeds in being released from

	the papal ban; rebellion of the barons, who choose Rudolf of Swabia as their 'anti-caesar'
1080	Henry IV banned again, has Clement III elected as his 'anti-pope'; death of Rudolf
1095	Pope Urban II puts forward proposal for a Crusade to liberate Jerusalem
1122	Concordate of Worms seals a truce in the contest between Emperor and Papacy
1138–1250	Hohenstaufen dynasty
1152–90	Frederick I (Barbarossa); revival of the fundamental conflict between Emperor and Pope and protracted wars with the powerful cities of Lombardy fighting for self-government, which they achieve with the Peace of Constance 1183
1159	Election of two popes and schism until 1177
1167	Henry 'the Lion', Duke of Saxony, conquers Pomerania
1186	Barbarossa's son Henry married to the heiress of the kingdom of Sicily
1194	Henry VI crowned King of Sicily. Height of imperial power
1197	Death of Henry VI.
1211–50	Frederick II. He spends most of his reign in Italy
1226	The Teutonic Order begins conquest and missionary work in Prussia
1231	*Statutum in favorem principum* concedes essential rights of the crown to princes. Northern Italian cities rise again against the Emperor
1237	Renewed conflict between Papacy and Emperor. Frederick excommunicated by Gregory IX (1239) and Innocent IV (1245)
1257	Double election of two 'foreigners', Richard, Earl of Cornwall and Alfonso, King of Castile, as emperors
1273–91	Rudolf I, the first Emperor of the Habsburg dynasty. With the acquisition of Austria and the duchies of Styria, Carinthia and Carniola, the foundations of future Habsburg power are created
1314–47	Ludwig I of Bavaria Emperor; dispute with Papacy resumed

1338	Electoral College rejects papal claims to confirmation of the Emperor
1346–78	Charles IV of Luxemburg builds up Bohemia as the basis of his power
1348	Foundation of the first German University at Prague
1348	The first wave of the Great Plague reaches Central Europe
1356	The *Golden Bull* finally fixes rules for imperial election
1368	Height of power of the Hanseatic League, whose fleet takes Copenhagen
1378–1417	Great Schism
1410–37	Sigismund I of Luxemburg Emperor
1414–17	Council of Constance to reunite and reform the Church
1438	Election of Albert II (d. 1439); from now on the Habsburg dynasty occupies a quasi-hereditary position within the Empire
About 1450	Johan Gutenberg invents the art of printing
1452	Frederick III the last German king to be crowned Emperor by the Pope in Rome
1493–1519	Emperor Maximilian I. His marriage policy lays the foundation for the world-wide power of the Habsburg dynasty
1517	Beginning of the Reformation. The monk Martin Luther (1483–1546) nails his 95 theses against the sale of indulgences to the door of Wittenberg's castle church
1519–56	Emperor Charles V. During his reign over his vast empire, including great parts of Italy and Spain with her American possessions, he aspired in vain to restore the Imperial Crown to its medieval supremacy
1521	Luther defends himself before the Imperial Diet at Worms, is banned but protected by the Saxon Elector; starts his translation of the Bible, rapid expansion of his gospel
1524–5	German Peasants' War
1530	Protestant princes at the Diet of Augsburg present a summary of their belief ('Confession of Augsburg')
1544	The newly founded order of the Jesuits, the vanguard of

the Counter-Reformation, gains its first foothold in Germany at Cologne

1545–63	Council of Trent provides doctrinal definitions and institutional structures for the Counter-Reformation
1555	After several wars between Protestant princes and the Emperor, at the Peace of Augsburg it is agreed that from now on every prince is to decide on the religion of his subjects ('*cuius regio, eius religio*')
1556	With the abdication of Charles V from now on the Spanish Kingdom and the Austrian Empire are ruled by different lines of the Habsburg dynasty.
1618–48	Thirty Years' War between Emperor and princes as well as between Catholics and Protestants. At the same time power struggle involving most European states
1640–88	Frederick William, the 'Great Elector' of Brandenburg, lays the foundations for the rise of Prussia
1648	Peace Treaty of Westphalia defines the outlines of the European order for the next century. Marks the ascendancy of France and the sovereignty of the German princes
1658	'Alliance of the Rhine' of western German princes with France against Habsburg
1661–1715	Personal rule of Louis XIV, King of France
1683–99	Habsburg's successful war against the Ottoman Empire by which it regains its status as one of Europe's leading powers
1692	The Duke of Brunswick becomes Elector of Hanover
1697	The Elector of Saxony is elected King of Poland
1701	The Elector of Brandenburg becomes King in Prussia
1701–14	War of the Spanish Succession: climax and turning point of French hegemony under Louis XIV. Bavarian alliance with France
1713–40	King Frederick William I of Prussia. Besides thorough reform of the central administration he raises the strength of the standing army to 83,000 men
1714	The Elector of Hanover inherits the English crown (George I)
1718	Treaty of Passarowitz; greatest extension of Austrian territory in the Balkans

1740–86	Frederick II (the Great) King of Prussia. In three wars against Austria and her allies Prussia rises to the status of a European Power
1756–63	Seven Years' War
1772	The first of three partitions of Poland (the others were 1793 and 1795) with gains for Prussia, Austria and Russia
1789	Outbreak of the French Revolution
1793	French armies occupy German territory west of the Rhine
1803	Secularization of the German ecclesiastical states to the benefit of those who lost lands on the left bank of the Rhine
1806	Sixteen princes of southern and western Germany form the Confederation of the Rhine in alliance with Napoleon. Formal dissolution of the Holy Roman Empire, Francis II assumes the rank of Emperor of Austria
1806–7	Prussia defeated by Napoleon; loses her western possessions and remains under French occupation
1807–14	Reforms in Prussia
1811	Foundation of the iron-mill of Krupp in Essen
1813–14	German 'Wars of Liberation' under Prussian leadership
1814–15	Congress of Vienna; peace settlement for Europe under the guidance of the Austrian Chancellor Metternich. Establishment of the German Confederation which takes the place of the Holy Roman Empire
1817	'Wartburg Festival' as first demonstration of German revolutionary nationalism
1819	Decrees of Karlsbad to protect German states from 'revolutionary' organizations and propaganda
1830	'July Revolution' in Paris
1832	Second great national demonstration at the 'Festival of Hambach'
1834	German Customs Union under Prussian leadership and excluding Austria. First German railway between Nuremberg and Fürth
1840	608 steam engines in Prussia, 223 in Austria.

1847	Karl Marx and Friedrich Engels publish *Communist Manifesto* in London
1848/49	German revolution. German Constitutional National Assembly in Frankfurt (May 1848–June 1849) draws up constitution for a future German Empire
1848	Prussian constitution promulgated
1849	King Frederick William IV of Prussia refuses German crown (3 April)
1850	Restoration of the German Confederation. Three-tier electoral law introduced in Prussia
1862	On the occasion of the constitutional conflict in Prussia Otto von Bismarck is appointed Prime Minister
1866	Prussia attacks and defeats Austria and her German allies in war for supremacy in Germany. North German Confederation under the leadership of Prussia
1870/71	Franco-Prussian war ends with the defeat of France and proclamation of the German *Reich* at Versailles
1873/74	Repressive laws against the Catholic Church (*Kulturkampf*)
1875	Foundation of the German Socialist Workers Party (later SPD)
1878	Anti-socialist laws
1881–84	Social insurance laws
1888–1918	Kaiser William II
1890	Dismissal of Bismarck. Large socialist gains in general elections
1896	First German navy law starts arms race with Britain
1912	SPD strongest party at general elections
1914–18	First World War
1917	USA declares war on Germany; revolution in Russia
1918	Armistice (11 November) and revolution in Germany. Abdication of the *Kaiser*. Germany becomes a republic
1919	Peace Treaty of Versailles; Constitution of the Weimar Republic
1923	Climax of inflation; Hitler's abortive putsch in Munich

1925	Treaty of Locarno as result of the foreign policy of Stresemann marks re-entry of Germany into the international community of nations. Hindenburg elected President
1929	Beginning of the world-wide economic crisis which hits Germany in 1930
1930	Dissolution of the last parliamentary government; from now on presidential cabinets ruling by decrees. Three million unemployed
1932	Last free elections, again a majority for anti- democratic parties (Hitler's NSDAP 33.5 per cent)
1933	Over six million out of work. 30 January Hitler appointed Chancellor. The totalitarian regime of Hitler and his party is based on the 'Enabling Law' of 24 March
1936	Olympic Games held in Berlin
1938	Annexation of Austria. Agreement with Britain, France and Italy in Munich over annexation of Czech border territories (*Sudetenland*). 9 November pogroms against the Jews
1939	Invasion and take-over of Czechoslovakia. August German–Soviet pact. 1 September attack on Poland, beginning of the Second World War
1940	German occupation of Denmark and Norway, the Netherlands and Belgium. 22 June capitulation of France. Hitler at the height of his power
1941	22 June beginning of the invasion of Russia. December Hitler declares war on the USA
1942	The *Wannsee* Conference decides on the execution of the programme for the extermination of the Jews
1942/43	Decisive defeat of the German army at the battle of Stalingrad
1944	20 July abortive attempt by high-ranking officers to assassinate Hitler
1945	30 April Hitler commits suicide. 7–8 May unconditional surrender of the German armed forces. Immediate loss of the territory east of Oder and Neisse. The rest of Germany divided into four zones of occupation
1945/46	Nuremberg trial against major Nazi war criminals

	Formation of *Länder* in all zones as units of administration. Foundation (CDU, SED, FDP) or reconstitution (SPD) of political parties
1947	East and West start drifting apart. Fusion of American and British zone with joint Economic Council. The Western zones are included into the Marshall Plan
1948	Currency reform in the Western zones. Russian blockade of West Berlin; constitutional assembly for West Germany
1949	Promulgations of the West German and East German Constitutions confirm the establishment of the Federal Republic of Germany (FRG) in the West and German Democratic Republic (GDR) in the East. After free elections in the FRG first coalition government under Chancellor Adenauer (CDU)
1952	Sovereignty granted to the FRG
1953	Abortive uprising in the GDR
1955	FRG joins NATO; GDR member of the Warsaw Pact. Sovereignty of the GDR proclaimed
1957	FRG founding member of the European Economic Community
1959	SPD drops Marxism when adopting the *Godesberg* programme
1961	Erection of the Wall which seals off West Berlin from the East
1963	Adenauer resigns, conservative governments continue in FRG
1968	Demonstrations all over West Germany (against the Vietnam War, for reforms at the universities etc.)
1969	SPD–FDP coalition government as result of federal elections
1971	In the GDR Walter Ulbricht forced to resign as head of the SED and is succeeded by Honnecker
1972	Basic Treaty between FRG and GDR as main result of the new *Ostpolitik*
1973	FRG and GDR join the United Nations.
1982	In the FRG, SPD-led coalition government loses majority and is succeeded by CDU/FDF administration under Kohl

1987	Honnecker's state visit to the FRG
1989	'Velvet' revolution in the GDR under the impact of Gorbachev's policy of reform in Russia. 9 November the Wall comes down
1990	3 October reunification of Germany when the GDR joins the FRG

Selected Further Reading

The list concentrates mainly on recent publications in English. Other works or articles should be traced through bibliographies in these books.

GENERAL

Fulbrook, M., *A Concise History of Germany* (Cambridge, 1990).
Kitchen, M., *The Cambridge Illustrated History of Germany* (Cambridge, 1996).
Schulze, H., *Germany: A New History* (Cambridge, MA, 1998).
Germany: A New Social and Economic History
    Vol. I: *1450–1630*, ed. R. W. Scribner (London, 1996).
    Vol. II: *1630–1800*, ed. S. Ogilvie (London, 1996).
    Vol. III: *Since 1800*, ed. S. Ogilvie and J. Overy (London, 1998).

MEDIEVAL GERMANY

Arnold, B., *Medieval Germany, 500–1300* (Basingstoke, 1997).
Du Boulay, F. R. H., *Germany in the Later Middle Ages* (London, 1983).
Fuhrmann, H., *Germany in the High Middle Ages* (Cambridge, 1986).
Haverkamp, A., *Medieval Germany, 1056–1273* (Oxford, 1988).
Reuter, T., *Germany in the Early Middle Ages, 800–1056* (London, 1991).
Scott, T., *Society and Economy in Germany, 1300–1600* (Basingstoke, 2002).

GERMANY FROM THE REFORMATION TO THE AGE OF THE FRENCH REVOLUTION

Asch, A. G., *The Thirty Years' War: The Holy Empire and Europe, 1618–1648* (Basingstoke, 1997).
Blanning, T. C. W., *The French Revolution in Germany* (Oxford, 1983).
Carsten, F. L., *The Origins of Prussia* (Oxford, 1954, 1982).
Dickens, A. G., *The German Nation and Martin Luther* (Glasgow, 1976).
Dwyer, P. G. (ed.), *The Rise of Prussia 1700–1830* (Harlow, 2000).
Evans, R. J. W., *The Making of the Habsburg Monarchy 1550–1700* (London, 1984).

Scott Dixon, C., *The Reformation in Germany* (Oxford, 2002).
Scribner, R. W., *The German Reformation*, 2nd edn (Basingstoke, 2003).
Vierhaus, R., *Germany in the Age of Absolutism* (Cambridge, 1988).

NINETEENTH-CENTURY GERMANY (1815–1918)

Berghahn, V., *Imperial Germany, 1871–1914: Economy, Society, Culture and Politics* (Cambridge, 1994).
Blackbourn, D., *The Fontana History of Germany, 1780–1918: The Long Ninetenth Century* (London, 1997).
Blackbourn, D. and Eley, D., *The Peculiarities of German History* (Oxford, 1985).
Breuilly, J., *Austria, Prussia and Germany, 1806–1871* (London, 2002).
Chickering, R., *Imperial Germany and the Great War, 1914–1918* (1998).
Feuchtwanger, E., *Bismarck* (London, 2002).
Sheehan, J., *German History 1770–1866* (Oxford, 1989).
Simms, B., *The Struggle for Mastery in Germany, 1779–1850* (Basingstoke, 1998).
Stadelmann, R., *Social and Political History of the German 1848 Revolution* (Ohio University Press, 1975).
Wehler, H.-U., *The German Empire 1871–1918* (Leamington Spa, 1985).

TWENTIETH-CENTURY GERMANY

Berghahn, V., *Modern Germany*, 2nd edn (Cambridge, 1987).
Bessel, R., *Germany after the First World War* (Oxford, 1993).
Beyme, K. von, *The Political System of the Federal Republic of Germany* (Aldershot, 1986).
Dahrendorf, R., *Society and Democracy in Germany* (London, 1968).
Fulbrook, M., *Anatomy of a Dictatorship: Inside the GDR, 1945–1989* (Oxford, 1995).
Fulbrook, M., *History of Germany 1918–2000: The Divided Nation*, 2nd edn (Oxford, 2002).
Hildebrand, K., *The Third Reich* (London, 1984).
Hillgruber, A., *Germany and Two World Wars* (London, 1981).
Jarausch, K., *The Rush to German Unity* (Oxford, 1994).
Kolb, E., *The Weimar Republic* (London, 1988).
Jeffries, I. and Melzer, M. (eds), *The East German Economy* (London, 1987).
Kershaw, I., *The Nazi Dictatorship*, 4th edn (London, 2000).
Kettenacker, L., *Germany since 1945* (Oxford, 1997).
Kramer, A., *The West German Economy 1945–1955* (Oxford, 1991).
Nicholls, A. J., *The Bonn Republic: West German Democracy, 1945–1990* (Oxford, 1995).
Noakes, J. and Pridham, G. (eds), *Nazism,* 4 vols (Exeter, 1983–98).

Index

200

Napoleon Bonaparte, emperor of the
French, 76–82, 84, 86
nation (German), 1, 6, 10, 29, 42,
72–4, 81, 86, 90, 92, 94–8,
111, 116, 135, 136, 166, 178
nationalism (German), 1, 12, 33,
53, 74, 89, 99, 117, 119,
120, 134, 139, 141, 169, 184
nation-state (German), 1, 12, 26,
27, 29, 42, 43, 73, 82–4, 90,
99, 106, 108, 110, 117, 127,
128, 161–3, 180, 183, 184
political, 9, 29, 33, 38, 167
NATO (North Atlantic Treaty
Organization), 166, 180, 181
Netherlands (Holland, Dutch
Republic), 20, 47, 49, 52, 53,
61, 62, 85, 121, 152
Nicholas II, Pope (1058–61), 15
Nicolai, Friedrich, author
(1733–1811), 73
nobility (aristocracy), 7–10, 13, 15,
17, 21, 22, 55, 56, 58, 59, 61,
70, 80, 86, 90, 92, 104, 105,
173
imperial knights, 19, 20, 28, 37,
53, 77
princes, 18, 19, 24–6, 28, 29, 32,
76, 83, 85, 88, 94, 158
Prussian (*Junker*), 70, 80, 87, 104,
105, 173
Nordic War, 63, 69
Norway, 152
NSDAP (National Socialism, Nazis),
132, 136, 137, 140–5, 148,
149, 168, 169, 174, 175, 183
Nuremberg, city, 24, 27, 38, 64, 102,
150
Laws, 157
war crimes trial at, 168

Oberländer, Theodor, minister in
Adenauer's government, 168
occupation (allied), zones of, 162–8
Oder, river, 49, 72
Osiander, Andreas, Protestant
reformer (1492–1552), 38

Osnabrück, city, 1, 48, 52, 84
see also Westphalian Peace Treaty
Otto, Bishop of Freising (1112–58),
6
Otto I, Emperor (936–73), 8, 9, 13

Pacific islands, 119
Palatinate (Rhineland), 9, 90
electorate, 29, 45, 46, 59
upper, 62
Palermo, city, 10
Palestine, 158
papacy (popes), 3, 12, 14–16, 18, 27,
31–3, 36, 41
Papen, Franz von, German
Chancellor (1879–1969), 137,
145
Paris, 9, 24, 75, 76, 86, 90, 93, 95,
120
commune, 115
parliament (representative
assemblies), 80, 86–8, 92, 93,
96, 117, 125, 159
National Assembly (1848), 94–7,
112, 124
Reichstag (1871–1918), 109–111,
113, 114, 116, 121, 122, 124
Nationl Assembly (1919), 124,
125, 135
Reichstag (1919–45), 126, 136,
137, 143, 144, 159
Bundestag FRG, 165, 167, 168
Prussian, 105
parliamentary government, 99, 114,
116, 121–4, 135
parties, political, 93, 96, 112, 113,
115–17, 124, 126, 131, 136,
142–4, 167
Centre Party, 112–14, 116, 122,
123, 125, 135, 136, 144, 146,
167
CDU (Christian Democratic
Union), 167–9, 173, 178
Conservative, 111, 113, 144
DDP (German Democratic Party),
125, 134, 135, 144
DNVP (National German People's
Party), 135, 137, 144

943
WEN

Wende, Peter.

A history of
Germany.

4/05

$26.95

DATE			

BAKER & TAYLOR